TO LIVE AGAIN

TO LIVE AGAIN

The Medical Miracle of Joe Philion

MARTYN KENDRICK

RANDOM HOUSE
TORONTO

Published in Canada in 1990 by Random House of Canada
Limited

Cataloguing in Publication Data

Kendrick, Martyn, 1953-
  To live again

ISBN 0-394-22126-5

1. Philion, Joey, 2. Burns and scalds in
children — Treatment. 3. Shriners Burns Institute
(Boston, Mass.). 4. Burns and scalds — Patients —
Biography. I. Title

RD96.4.K4 1989   362.1'9711'0924   C89-094460-1

Jacket design: Falcom Design & Communications Inc.
Jacket photographs: Joe, Courtesy of the Philion family
                    Hospital scene, Gabe Palmer/Masterfile
Author photograph: Studio 110

Printed and bound in Canada

To Joe.

ACKNOWLEDGMENTS:

I would like to thank Linda and Mike, Nia and her family, Wayne, Father Michael, Anne and Camille, Cheri, and Tim (alias Santa Claus) and Marino. Many thanks to my agent, Larry Hoffman, who helped steer me through some particularly difficult periods in the writing. Ed Carson opened up some creative doors, which considerably balanced out the manuscript. As ever, I am grateful to my wife, Lucille, whose patience and companionship even during manic moments around deadlines is greatly appreciated.

TO LIVE AGAIN

MOTHER'S MESSAGE

I was not prepared for what happened to my son Joe. I was
not prepared to watch my child, who had sacrificed himself
to save his brother and myself, hover near death, racked with
pain even morphine could not touch. I was not prepared to
see his strong and supple body transformed into a piece of raw
flesh; festering, swollen, bleeding and blistered, burned beyond
imagining. I was not prepared for the days that dragged into
months that seemed like years when my son would beg me not
to let them move him an inch, the pain was too much, and
I had to explain that they must. They moved him constantly.

There were so many times I wanted to take him in my arms,
but even to touch him caused pain. I let my hair gently fall
over his body in place of an embrace. I knew only that if Joey
lived I would be happy. If he died I would be nothing, not
even sad. I would be empty, or there would be agonizing
memories of what was once my life.

Nearly everything I have lived through these past two years

has been just below the threshold of thought. My life resided as much in my son Joe as in me, a life bond that couldn't be broken by my confused thoughts or overwhelming fears. Whenever that bond was shaken, whenever someone sought to disrupt it, I knew it in my guts and Joey knew it in his.

I begged God, I bargained, I wept and prayed, and I believed — despite medical opinions — that Joey was going to live. He did. We did.

Tens of thousands of people the world over have shared in Joey's grief and victories and have been moved by his courage during and after the fire that destroyed ninety-five percent of his body. I shall never forget sitting at the head of Joey's bed in Boston's Shriners Institute, calling out to him, asking him to hang on just a little longer. I shall never forget the letters of support, thousands of them, that were sent to Joey. As I read them to him, I felt my voice becoming stronger, as if all the voices of the people who had been touched were being channeled through me. A will much larger than my own was calling Joey from the brink of death back to life. Those letters and a generosity of spirit, which we will never forget, changed our family's tragedy into something extraordinarily meaningful. I believed then that there was perhaps a purpose in Joey's experience. I believe that even more now.

Joey has often asked why people have responded to his story. I have tried to explain. He has often said he wished he had a way of paying them back and thanking them.

It is because of this that we decided to share Joey's story.

It is because of this that we smile at one another through our sorrow.

CHAPTER ONE

Joey sat on the edge of the rock bed, silent, watching, listening. His eyes scanned the islands in the distance. Seals lounged on the rocks to his left, sunning, occasionally calling out to one another or flopping haphazardly into the water.

The water. Endlessly it rolled toward him, and endlessly it rolled back again. Endlessly it crashed against the rocks, and he watched, fascinated. His eyes followed the crest of a breaking wave down to the right side of the inlet. He saw something. Killer whale, he said to himself, though he didn't like the name "killer." It didn't seem to fit somehow. There was the whale, not half a mile away, and then another and another, riding the waves, leaping. He loved the whales.

But not the sharks, at least not in the same way.

You wondered about whales. You wondered what they'd do if you swam out and hung onto their tails. You wondered about their singing and the grace and speed with which their

enormous, glistening bodies moved through the water. You
didn't wonder about the tails of sharks. Sharks were part of
the cycle of eating and dying on the shores of Vancouver Island.
Sharks were caught and cut open from end to end with a knife
in your hand and fear in your belly. In the shark's belly were
the baited hooks, which cost five bucks. Fearless fishermen
would reach into the mouth or belly and retrieve them. Joey
and his friends would ride in the rowboat and watch for hours,
fascinated and afraid, when the kill was on. Other sharks would
come in, smelling the blood running into the cold blue water,
causing the water to rage for a time as a fury of sharp-toothed
jaws ripped apart the dead sharks, then disappeared into the
ocean.

Joey turned his eyes from the water and scanned the
shoreline for his brother Danny. Danny was afraid of the
sharks. He didn't want to be, but the sight of their gaping jaws
and wide attacking bodies and the smell of death were too much
for him. The fear overwhelmed the fascination he felt. Joey
saw Danny racing along the shore, stopping here and there
to pick up something. Joey knew he would hesitate at the edge
of the rock bed, his refuge against the water, which housed
the sharks and other unknown terrors that stuck to your skin,
sucked the life out of you and pulled you down to the ocean
floor. Then, gathering his courage, Danny hopped onto the
rock bridge and shuffled across to Joey, his brother, his other
refuge against the unknown.

Joey turned and raised his eyes to the skies. The sky above
him was misty white. Over the mountains, way off in the
distance, dark storm clouds were forming. He imagined blue
sky pierced by shafts of brilliant light falling down into the
mountains and the water, dawn skies and dusk and the stars
that hurtled through space in the night.

Joey loved the sky. Then his eyes alighted on his favorite
of all the wild creatures, the bald eagle. He watched as the
lord of the skies tipped its wing, took the wind under it and,

sailing on hidden currents, circled down and down until the white of its wings became visible.

Joey was hovering thousands of feet above the earth when Danny reached him. He pointed up into the sky, following the slow, spiraling descent with his finger. And the water and the rocks and the terror of the unknown were lost as Danny followed the flight of the eagle with the wind across the sun and the sky and the water. . . .

As Joey looked upon Danny, he laughed, because he loved his little brother as much as he loved the effortless power of the eagle above them. "One day," he said, "you'll see me up there, Danny. One day I'm going to be flying just like that eagle." And they sat there together, laughing, watching the eagle until it became a shadow upon the sun and vanished into the horizon.

Linda Hawkins loved the wilderness. She loved fishing and campfires and the lonely cry of the loon across the lake. She hadn't thought of living in the wilderness until Mike came along. Mike was five feet nine, blond, blue eyed, outgoing. They met through Linda's ex-husband, Andy Philion, in the summer of 1983.

It was Mike who would tell her tales of the west coast, of the whales, of the wind howling through the trees and the ocean roaring. He had spent most of his life there and found comfort in nature. He didn't like the city. His parents had separated when he was young and, though he saw them occasionally, his family wasn't close.

Nature called out to him, gave him solace. His stories revived Linda's love of nature. She began to think that nothing could be more beautiful than the western Canadian wilderness Mike described.

Joey and Danny loved his stories, too. Joey was eleven then, four feet tall, with blond wavy hair, blue eyes, a strong body, a quiet, cheerful disposition and a dimpled smile. Danny, three years younger and a foot shorter, was the more boisterous and unpredictable of the two. You never quite knew what Danny would do next. The four of them did everything together. With Mike, they imagined that life was nothing more than lying on a beach, watching a falling star, fishing for salmon off the rocks of Vancouver Island, running along the sand, listening to the songs of the whales while the sun drenched your body in glorious, soothing hot light.

Linda and Mike were married in May 1985. One week later, Linda, who had never been away from Toronto without her family for any length of time, found herself enthusiastically agreeing with Mike that they should go west. They packed their belongings into a fresh-off-the-line mobile home, which Mike had managed to finagle through a drive-away company, and headed west.

Along the way, Mike told them stories about the places they were passing. They loved the rugged interior of Ontario's northern townships, with their enormous rock beds and glacially formed lakes that hugged the land like outstretched fingers. They were awed by the lightning storms in the prairies, the farms the size of small cities. But it was the mountains that captured the boys' imagination. To Joey, these were the mountains of Canadian fable, massive peaks stretching across Colorado, over the borders into Alberta and way up into the vast interior of British Columbia. Beyond that he had dim visions of a barren tundra that stretched on for unknowable distances into the icy Arctic, and icebergs as big as cargo ships.

They stopped in Banff and Jasper, two mountain towns that welcomed tourists and bears just about equally. Mike showed them some places where he had worked and told them what they could expect over the next hill or around the next curve. In Vancouver they dropped off the mobile home, unpacked their meager belongings, boarded the ferry and headed to Vancouver Island. They ended their journey in Campbell River.

It was everything Mike had said it would be, wild and natural. The ocean roared. The mountains surrounded them in the near distance. The boys fished and raised rabbits, made friends and built tree forts. They took to the landscape as if it were their own backyard. In "God's country," as Mike called it, Joey fell in love with the eagles, proud and majestic birds that circled above the ocean and mountains, then perched overhead in the branches of the largest trees. He developed a desire to fly.

Mike and Linda drove taxi for awhile, and Mike found odd jobs, enough to keep them going. They didn't need much. They caught salmon, raised chickens, traded and bartered.

In September Mike said he knew of a place some miles inland. He said he wanted to be even more secluded. So the family packed their belongings into the beat-up Datsun they had bought and moved down the coast. They stayed till well into the fall, but with no money and few provisions they began thinking seriously about the winter. They couldn't stay. They considered moving to Vancouver, but they thought it would be easier to find work in Toronto, where they had family and friends. Within five years, they figured, they would be able to make enough money to return to the west coast and settle down.

They moved in with Linda's father and mother for a few months, and Mike and Linda found jobs at an express delivery company, Linda dispatching and Mike delivering. But there was little privacy at home, so Mike found them an apartment. In return for superintending, they lived free of charge. That lasted less than a year.

Mike had lived in Huntsville, Ontario, when he was younger, and he remembered it fondly. It was a small community with time for the simpler aspects of life. The woods were close and the water was clean. It was the kind of place where you got to know the baker and the butcher, where you could maintain an account at the local hardware store. They scoured the area and stumbled upon a small, L-shaped cottage just nine miles outside Orillia. It wasn't much, but it was affordable and they could see the potential.

It was just off the highway in a little cluster of cottages on Cleveland Avenue. It wasn't exactly private, but Lake Couchiching was just down the road, and there were lots of kids, which was great for the boys. With substantial help from Linda's father they put a down payment together and less than two weeks later moved into their new home. That was in March 1987.

It was difficult to decide where to begin. Everything needed immediate attention. New plumbing, new wiring, new furnace, new roof, siding, insulation — the list went on and on. Joey was overjoyed. In the morning he would ask Mike, "So what's next, what's next?" It was his first real home and he wanted it to be beautiful and he wanted to say that he had helped. Linda remembers watching when he and Mike were repairing the roof. Mike didn't want him to help, but Joey insisted. He would pick up one of the fifty-pound bundles of shingles, heave it over his shoulder and haul it up the ladder to the roof. Linda was proud of him. "He was only fourteen," she explains, "and here he was laying down a roof like a grown man."

Joey shrugged off her praise. "It's gotta be done, Mom," he said, "and somebody's gotta do it."

During the evenings the family would sit around a campfire and relax. Mike and Linda are a fairly private couple and liked to spend time with the family. But they met the neighbors quickly, and everyone was friendly. Friends and family often visited for the weekend to sit around the campfire and enjoy steaks and a cold beer or two.

Slowly, as the humid summer months passed, they saw their modest little dream house coming together. Much still needed to be completed, but with winter approaching and the boys getting ready for school, Mike wanted to finish only what was necessary to prepare for winter. Then he'd get a job in town, and they would settle in for the winter. They bought as much insulation as they thought they would need to insulate the inside and the outside of the house.

Early in the summer Mike had thrown out the oil furnace and replaced it with an electrical one, which he had picked up inexpensively. But when they went to put the new furnace in, Mike discovered that he would need a two-hundred-ampere system, and the house was set up with only a one-hundred-amp system. The necessary changes would be costly and time-consuming. With only a few weeks before the cold set in, the house was without heat. Mike went out and bought a wood stove. He hoped that with the wood stove, the fireplace and extra insulation, he could wait until the following spring to install central heating.

There wasn't much choice, really. The little money they had started with had been eaten up by the extensive renovations. They owed thousands of dollars in bills, and a mortgage. The house would have to wait.

In October they experienced the first biting cold of an Orillia winter. The tiny cottage barely kept out the wind, let alone the cold. They would huddle around their temperamental fireplace for warmth. Mike had started work at Vulcan Hart Industries, a manufacturing plant about nine miles down the road. He was up at five and on the road by six to hitchhike to work each morning. At that point they didn't have a car, and the strained family budget just wouldn't allow for one in the near future.

The month of October was only a glimmer of what was to come. In November, the howling winds, the bitter northern cold and the snow came at them furiously.

Mike would get up reluctantly, wearily, and get the fireplace and potbelly stove ready. Then Linda would get up and, shivering in the early dawn, make him some breakfast and prepare a lunch. Mike would walk about a quarter of a mile to the junction, then wait for some good Samaritan to give him a lift. Sometimes he waited only a minute or two, sometimes as long as an hour. When the cold came, no amount of clothing would protect him. On one occasion when he arrived at work — he always made it on time for the seven o'clock shift — the driver who picked him up wanted to take him to the hospital. His face looked frostbitten. His boss sent him home.

Linda would get the fires going nicely before the boys got up, and she made breakfast while they prepared for school. At eight fifteen they got on the bus. Linda would wave good-bye. She didn't see any of them again until around four o'clock.

In the house, she would sit before the fireplace trying to keep warm. The only place the family could keep warm was by the fire. They had already used up nearly a cord of wood, which Mike and Joey had chopped and stacked neatly outside the house. It wasn't going to be enough, she could see that — at this rate it would only last until early December. And wood was $150 a cord. It was going to bite into an already over-stretched budget.

The pipes broke for the first time early in November. Mike and Linda awoke at around 4:00 AM. They could hear a muffled hissing sound. Still sleepy, Linda thought it sounded like snakes in the house. It wasn't a big house so it didn't take long for Mike to discover what was causing the noise. The pipes had burst underneath the sink, and water was leaking all over their nicely tiled kitchen floor. Mike shut off the water, cleaned up the mess and tried to locate the leak. By the time he found it, it was nearly time for him to go to work and for Linda to get up.

After Mike left, she sat down in the ice-covered kitchen, thinking life might be like this all winter. Mike had said to leave the water off until he had made a thorough examination of the pipes. That meant no water for dishes or for a morning wash or for coffee. When he got home at four-thirty he crawled under the house, maneuvered through the crawl space with a propane torch, thawed the main pipe and soldered it back together. Then he wrapped the pipes with insulation and hoped.

The boys thought it was great fun. They were in the house listening for Mike's commands. "Okay, Joey, turn on the main switch. . . . No, turn it off, turn it off. Okay, now wait till I call you." Mike didn't think it was fun at all. It took three hours. He was exhausted, freezing and hungry. That night the family crowded around the fire after dinner, sitting close, each of them lost in thought. Mike broke the silence. "This is going to be one hell of a winter, guys."

Two days later the pipes burst again. Linda heard the muffled creaking sound. She didn't call Mike at work. When he got home she didn't have the heart to tell him about it. She didn't have to. Before she had a chance to say anything he had gone to the sink. There were icicles hanging from the faucet. He broke them and turned on the water. Nothing. "I remember that day clearly," says Linda. "When I came back into the kitchen he looked at me, crestfallen. 'Again?' he asked. I tried to make light of it."

By the end of the winter the job of thawing and rewrapping the pipes had become so routine they could do it in less than an hour. When Joey and Danny came home from school, they would go straight to their rooms and put on the thick wool pants and heavy socks they wore in the house. They all kept their coats on.

By the end of December the pipes had burst twenty-eight times. Mike would come home, grab the propane torch, crawl under the house and repair them. There wasn't always enough time to finish the dishes, wash and bathe. Baths were excruciating even when the water was running and hot because the bathroom was so cold. Occasionally Mike and Linda would take the kids out to McDonald's for a respite, but more frequently they sat huddled around the fire.

Danny and Joey were doing well despite the hardships. Joey was going off to dances with his friends, meeting a girl here and there. He liked school but didn't do so well academically. He didn't like math and wasn't that thrilled with English, either, and he needed special help in those areas. But he could do anything with his hands. He was polite, a bit shy, determined, helpful and, although he was not studious, he was a good worker. Teachers would comment to Linda that he was a special boy.

He had also developed a strong friendship with Wayne Cooke, a boy his own age who, like Joey, dreamed of flying and loved to tinker with bikes. Wayne was introduced to Joey by Wayne's father, who was Mike's foreman at Vulcan Hart Industries.

Joey could rattle off the name of almost any plane you could show him. He and Wayne spent hours reading and discussing the content of aviation magazines. Wayne had been in Air Cadets for nearly a year and suggested to Joey that he join. Linda thought it might be expensive, but as Wayne's mother, Lynn, explained, the cadets cost nothing to join. Joey was ecstatic.

When Joey first got his uniform, he pressed it till the creases were like knives and shined his shoes till he could see his face in them. Then he proudly walked into the living room. (Later, Mike showed him how to shine his shoes even better.) On the first night Joey was to attend a meeting, Wayne Sr. said he would pick Joey up at home and drive Joey and Wayne to the hall. But Joey walked from his Cumberland beach home to Wayne's house, obviously proud of the uniform. "I didn't want to put you out," he said.

Before Joey got his uniform, Linda spent approximately $150 on a suit he could wear to cadets. But what really excited Joey was his watch. She had bought him a three-dollar watch, more for show than anything else, but Joey thought it was awesome. He would adjust his sleeve to show the watch, and every few minutes he would sneak a glance at it and smile.

He fit into cadets easily. He already knew many of the planes by name, and among other young hopefuls he was as close as he was going to get for a while to the pilots who commanded his respect. He loved the drills, the precision exercises, the camaraderie. He and Wayne talked of the planes they would one day be flying. Given the way he carried himself and the pride with which he wore his uniform, Linda was sure he was going to do something great, perhaps become a great pilot or one of the high-ranking officers whose discipline and courage he admired.

In February 1988, Joey persuaded Linda to let him sign up for gliding lessons with Wayne. It didn't take much to persuade her. He had wanted to go gliding ever since he was a young boy. Gliding, he said, would be as close as he would get to soaring with the eagles.

Cadets, common dreams and motorcycles cemented the boys' friendship. Wayne and Joey worked daily on an old bike Joey's grandfather had bought at an auction. Joey had been determined to get it working before he met Wayne, and Wayne matched his determination. It was a homemade power bike that reached up to forty-five sputtering miles per hour when they finally got it working. They rode it up and down the street in front of Joey's house.

When they weren't working on the bike, they would head out over the frozen lake toward an island about a quarter mile offshore and go ice fishing, or they would walk the trails and country roads close to their home. Often Joey would sleep at Wayne's home. Joey couldn't reciprocate — it was too cold at his house. "Wait until the summer, Wayne," he said, "and then you can sleep over and we'll have everything fixed for next year."

When Danny saw his older brother in his uniform, he immediately wanted to join the air cadets, but he was too young. Later, Danny, Linda would tell him. And she meant it, although she wondered if he did. She thought the discipline would be good for him.

Linda explains the difference between Danny and Joey by way of an example. If you asked Joey to go to the store, he'd be gone within a minute and return immediately. He enjoyed being of service to people. Danny, on the other hand, would start by asking for a quarter and finally demand a dollar before he agreed to go — if he did — and then he'd be gone for an hour or more, having met some friends along the way. More likely than not he'd return with the wrong item or nothing at all and no money in his pocket. They were as different as night and day.

Toward the end of that first November, Linda decided to look for work in Toronto. It was impossible for her to work in Orillia without a car, and it was hard to watch Mike leave every morning to walk through freezing cold or blizzard to earn a paycheck that barely paid for the family's needs. Linda sat at home, wrapped in a blanket, waiting for her men to return to a freezing house. "Often," she says, "it was so cold I couldn't prepare dinner. I couldn't stand it. So I told Mike one day I was leaving. I was going to Toronto, and when I'd made enough money to buy a car, I'd be back. He wouldn't hear of it. What about the boys? What about you alone in Toronto? What about this and that? He told me later he'd felt that somehow his manhood was on the line. He'd felt that my working was taking away from his role as provider. But I had made up my mind. I explained it to the boys, and I left the next morning."

She worked for five weeks in Toronto and earned enough

to buy another used Datsun. Her father helped pay for the insurance. She returned home just before Christmas with the car filled with groceries.

It did get easier, though not much. Linda drove Mike to work, so he never had to freeze on the highway again, and she got a job at a local restaurant. They had a bit more money coming in, but the wood and the mortgage and the bills and the continually bursting pipes ate away at their dwindling resources.

Another blow came when Mike brought their insurance agent in to look at the flood damage caused by the bursting pipes. It was the third week in February 1988. The agent looked the house over and said there was nothing the insurance company could do because the house wasn't properly prepared for winter. Mike explained about the electric furnace in the shed and the fact that they didn't have the time or money to get it installed. The insurance agent sympathized but explained again that his company could do nothing for them under the circumstances.

A few days later the insurance agent phoned to ask if he could drop by. It wouldn't take much time, he said. Linda and Mike hoped the insurance company had found a way to cover the damages, but that wasn't exactly what the insurance agent had in mind.

Not only could the company not assume liability for the damages, they had to cancel the insurance policy. Because of its electrical system — one hundred rather than two hundred amperes — the house was unsafe. If the family tried to use all their existing electrical appliances at once, they could over-burden the system. Mike explained, but to no avail.

Mike and Linda were beyond anger. They had no money to speak of, an unsafe house, no insurance, icy floors and a furious northern winter to contend with. It was a bleak family that went to bed that night.

Over the course of the next week they tried to find a better perspective. "We saw that we had made it through this far, and if we could just put up with another two months at the most we would get over it," Linda explained. "We could beat the winter, and through the spring and summer we could put the house together just as we had originally planned. We would have made it. It couldn't possibly have gotten any worse."

That was at the end of February.

CHAPTER TWO

Mike struggled as he always did to forget that the alarm was telling him to get up and get ready for work. He stumbled into the bathroom, groggy and shivering but relieved to find that the pipes had not burst. Linda rolled over, seeking the warmth that had left the bed when Mike got up. She didn't want to get up and face the chill of the room. Once outside the bed, it would be a good while before she felt warm again. She wrapped the blankets around her even tighter.

Then, bracing herself, she got up and dressed quickly. She walked across the living room and checked on the boys. They were still asleep.

Mike was calling out. "Linda, where are my other socks, man? Didn't you just wash them?" Mike was always losing his socks.

"Look beside the dresser, in the hamper there," she answered, as she peered into the fridge. It's probably warmer in there than it is out here, she thought, as she began laying out the lunches and preparing breakfast.

At 6:40 Linda called to Mike that she was ready anytime. As was their routine, Mike warmed up the car while Linda stacked the wood stove and the fireplace with kindling. She would drive Mike to work, return home, then light the fires and warm the house before getting the boys up. She checked to see if there were any hot coals. The stove was cold to the touch. She left the stove door ajar, checked the boys once more and ran out to the car. It was 6:45 as she and Mike pulled out of the driveway.

Approximately ten minutes later Joey woke up to the smell of smoke. Then he saw the flames. "Danny," he screamed. "Danny, get up! Fire!" Danny was still sleeping. "Danny, Danny, get up. Get out of here. Fire." Joey could see Danny stumble out of bed and race out the door. Joey wanted to go, too, but what about his mother? Where was she?

Restraining the urge to flee, Joey returned to the living room and began calling desperately for his mother. The living room, which separated him from his mother's room, was a wall of flames. He kept screaming for his mother as the flames and the smoke swirled menacingly toward him. He was choking and crying. "Mom," he screamed, as he charged through the flames across the living room to his mother's room. He rushed inside. She wasn't there. He was on fire now, and terrified. There was only one way out — back through the flames that were edging through the doorway of his mother's room. He hesitated, then raced once again through the living room to his bedroom, hoping to escape through the bedroom window. As he rushed through the door he tripped and sprawled on the floor. His clothes were in flames. He grabbed a blanket off his bed and wrapped it around himself.

He wanted to get up, but he couldn't. He remembered from somewhere in his past that you were supposed to stay low in a fire because heat rose. "Stay low," he kept repeating to himself as he lay on the floor, the flames spreading all around him. The fire was licking at his feet and swirling around him. He was trapped by the intense heat, the flames and the noise, the relentless hissing of the attacking fire. He tried to become smaller and curled into a fetal position. "Somebody help me please, please help me," he cried. He doesn't remember how long he lay there. He only knows that he was terrified, paralyzed with fear, when he looked down at his feet. He could see the flames engulfing the blanket where his feet used to be.

"I wanted to die then and just get out of it. I just lay there and thought, this is it. And then I thought of my mom. And then I thought, maybe if I stay here someone will come and rescue me, so I did. I just lay there waiting for I don't know how long. Then something in my mind told me to get up and I did and I ran to my back window and tried to smash it. I couldn't so I got the lamp at the side of my bed and began smashing it out. Then I began crawling out but got stuck and I could feel my legs burning in the fire behind me and I screamed and screamed but nobody heard me and I finally managed to kind of rock my body through the window until I had enough room to pull myself through and fall down outside the house."

He was engulfed in flames and bleeding from the shards of glass that lacerated his body as he rocked himself out the window. His jeans were on fire. Joey rolled in the snow. Not three yards away from him, the house continued to burn furiously.

Linda Young, the Hawkins' next-door neighbor, ran outside, frantic. Danny had just run into her house. He was safe, but he was crying out about his brother and his mother. She couldn't quite make out what he was saying. She could see the billowing flames not twenty feet away, and she was afraid. She saw a ball of flames leaping and rolling on the ground outside the Hawkins house. She ran toward it, knowing but not wanting to that this ball of flames was a human being. As she reached Joey's side she drew back involuntarily,

repulsed by the quivering mass of burning flesh that Joey
Philion had become.

There was desperate terror and pain in his eyes. Later Linda
Young would say she couldn't believe it was a human being
she was looking at. Joey was black, and smoke was pouring
out of his mouth, his eyes, his ears. His pants were still in
flames. He was wheezing and moaning, pleading for help. She
found herself acting in spite of herself. His clothes and the
blanket he was wrapped in were burning, so she began packing them with snow. Not enough. Joey was screaming, moaning. "My legs, my feet, please help me. Please stop the fire
on my legs."

She grabbed his burning jeans and began pulling them off.
As she pulled, his skin was peeling away. They were so hot
the zipper melted into his thigh. She managed to get them down
to his ankles. Frantically she pulled harder, afraid that she
might pull the feet off along with them. She couldn't get them
off. They are going to burn right through him, she thought,
struggling. I must get them off.

After a mighty struggle she managed to pull the jeans over
Joey's ankles and throw them. They landed on the wooden
seat of an old swing set, which moments later burst into flames.

Joey was lying naked, the blanket he'd covered himself with
wrapped around his smoking body. Linda used the blanket
to pull Joey away from the intense heat of the house. She continued to pack snow around Joey's charred body. Wherever
she touched him, his skin came off in her hands. She was
frantic.

Out in front, the neighbors had gathered. Everyone was
trying to help in some way, but the fire had gone too far. Two
neighbors, Doug and Rick, noticed the car was gone, so they
figured Mike and Linda were probably gone, too. Danny was
okay. He was standing over at the Youngs' house, looking confused and scared. But what about Joey? Had someone called
an ambulance?

At about 7:05, Linda Hawkins noticed smoke drifting across the highway. It seemed to be in the vicinity of her street. She had seen the fire trucks pass, heard the sirens screaming, but she thought nothing of it — she had other things to think about. She had to get the boys off to school, do some errands around the house, then get herself ready for work. The fire trucks had their work to do, and she had hers. But as she drove closer, it became clear the fire was on her street.

As she turned onto Cleveland Avenue she knew with gut-wrenching clarity that it was her house. She screamed as the shock began to set in, and she steeled herself for the next harrowing moments.

Cars, people, smoke, and voices everywhere. She could see Rick and Wilma and Doug running frantically around the front of the house. She tried to run in through the front door, but the smoke and flames drove her back. She searched for signs of Joey and Danny. She was beside herself with fear. Then she saw Danny standing on Linda's porch and turned toward him. At that moment she heard for the first time the labored screams coming from behind the house. She could make out Linda's voice, though not the words. Thank God Danny's all right, she thought as she ran past him. "Danny, stay there, don't come out."

As she turned the corner at the back of the house she could see Linda struggling with something. Even before she could see clearly through the smoke she knew it was Joey. She heard herself moaning as she ran. "Please God, no, please, oh, my God, no, not this. . . ." He was beyond recognition. As she touched him, tried to hold him close to her breast to comfort him, his flesh came off in her hands. She was crying, saying over and over again, "Joey, I'm so sorry, my poor Joey, I'm so sorry." Linda Young had moved back to allow Linda to get close. They were both crying. Joey was conscious the whole time, and he looked up at his mother, his eyes intent upon her face. "Mom, don't cry, Mom, I'm gonna be okay. I'm gonna be okay. It wasn't your fault. Are you okay, Mom? Where's Danny? Where's Mike?''

She sat there beside him crying, wanting to do or say something that would ease his pain. "Joey, it's going to be okay. The ambulance is coming, Joey, my poor, poor Joey.''

Linda noticed the smoke had clogged Joey's lungs. His breathing was labored. Linda hovered over him, chanting words of comfort, praying. They waited an agonizing thirty minutes for the ambulance.

Linda had to resist the urge to embrace him. She wanted to take the pain to herself, take it away from him, but she could do nothing. They waited.

Joey was moaning when the ambulance arrived, a slow, steady, desperate groan. He needed oxygen. His body was still smoking. The paramedics were unsure what to do. They doused him with water. They were reluctant to move him, fearing his body would fall apart. With difficulty they managed to get him onto a stretcher. They drove the nine miles to Orillia's Soldier's Memorial Hospital, Linda beside Joey, the oxygen mask covering the lower part of his face, his eyes looking up at Linda, pleading, or closed tightly as he concentrated on breathing.

There was pandemonium when they arrived at the hospital. Doctors, nurses and orderlies were preparing for the emergency. But no one was prepared for what they saw. None of them had ever seen anything like it. As they wheeled Joey into an emergency room, they debated about how best to move him. Like the paramedics, the orderlies and nurses were afraid Joey's body would fall apart if they moved him. The debate went on for minutes. Meanwhile Joey Philion, conscious, burned beyond recognition, racked with pain, with muscles and tendons destroyed in the fire, got up off his stretcher unassisted, walked over to the bed and lay down on it. Many people in the room believed he would die before he left that bed.

While the nurses were attempting to clean off the wounds,

Linda was pacing outside. She had called Mike and was desperate to see him. She had told him on the phone that it was deadly serious, that some people said Joey was going to die.

Prior to the call, Mike was not consciously aware of anything amiss. The firehall was right across from Vulcan Hart Industries, the factory where he and one hundred other Orillians worked; he'd become used to the sound of sirens charging out into the countryside. The switchboard operators had just started work when Linda called, and weren't sure where Mike was stationed. They would have to send someone to locate him. They were thinking about that when Mike walked up to the supervisor's office.

Mike says that about the time the call came, he felt an overwhelming need to walk from his work station. He wasn't sure just where he was going or why, but he headed directly for the supervisor's office. He was in a daze. As he approached the office, Gord, his supervisor, told him he had an important call to take. Gord had already had word of the fire.

Mike was frantic when he got off the phone. "I have to get down to the hospital right away," he said. "Joey's been hurt. I've got to be there."

"My car's waiting outside," Gord responded, "Let's go."

When they arrived at the hospital, Mike saw his wife and Linda Young. Both Mike and Linda began crying as they embraced. "How is he? What's going to happen? Can we see him? Are you okay? Where's Danny? And what about Kelly?" Nobody knew it then but Kelly, Joey's dog, had died in the fire.

Nobody had answers. Nobody knew what was going to happen. Linda, still reeling from the smell of her son's burned flesh, from the impact of the reality that was suddenly thrust upon her, explained that he looked bad. "They think he's going to die," she said. Mike looked lost. They just stood there crying, holding one another tightly, afraid that if either of them let go both of them would fall apart.

They waited. Periodically a nurse would come out, then a doctor, to explain that they were cleaning him off and still assessing the damage. The more the doctors saw, the more worried they became. One hour after Joey's arrival, it was clear to the doctors that their hospital was not equipped to deal with his condition. Dr. Toye, one of the attending doctors, had already performed a life-saving operation by making an incision in his side to reduce the pressure of the fluid that was building up and constricting his internal organs. That was all he could do. He wanted to transfer him to Toronto's Hospital for Sick Children. It had one of the best burn units in the country, the doctors assured Linda. If anyone was going to save Joey, it would be Sick Kids.

Linda and Mike signed the papers. A nurse came out to explain the procedure. "Linda," she said, "it may be too late. We may not be able to do anything for him. And maybe it's better that way." It was the first of many times when Linda would be told by medical staff that her son was going to die.

She began crying. "Leave me alone, please, don't say that. You don't know what you are saying. He's my son and he's not going to die. Can I see him? I must see him." The nurse was reluctant, because the staff had so much to do to prepare for the transfer. Linda insisted until she was allowed to see him for a moment. He was partially cleaned. But instead of looking better he looked worse. She could see just what the fire had done to his body, and she wavered for a moment. Maybe the nurse was right. Maybe Dr. Toye was right when he said, bluntly, "I'm afraid, Linda, that he's not going to make it. We don't have any choice but to transfer, but I can't honestly say that he's going to make it. He's burned bad, Linda." As she stood by Joey's bedside she tried to will herself into his mind, a mind she hoped shock had mercifully claimed for the moment. She heard her voice speaking her inmost thoughts. She was whispering to Joey. "Joey, we are going to meet you in Toronto where the doctor tells us you have to go. They will make you better there, Joey. But, Joey, you must fight. You have to fight harder than you've ever fought before. No matter what happens, you just fight, and we'll get through this. And Joey, I'll always be here, no matter what. Okay? No matter how long it takes, no matter what it costs, nothing matters more to me than you, and I'll be here to help you fight. I love you, Joey."

Joey nodded.

She wanted to touch him, but she couldn't. He'd already begun to swell. She felt faint as she stumbled to the waiting room. In the sea of faces, she found Mike. He and Wayne Cooke, foreman and friend, were figuring out what they would need for the trip to Toronto. They would have to return to the house to get the car. They would need clothes. They would have to make plans for Danny. They weren't sure about anything, because they didn't know what they were up against.

Wayne Jr., Joey's best friend, had left school and gone to the hospital. He was trying desperately to persuade the nurse to let him in to see Joey. By chance, as Joey was being transferred to the ambulance, they met in the hallway of the hospital. Joey was unconscious, and Wayne walked along beside him, looking with fear and amazement at his best friend.

In the waiting room, Wayne Sr. said to Mike, "Mike, don't worry about little things, we'll make sure those things you need are attended to. You just worry about getting yourself down to Toronto to help. I'll drive you back to the house to get the car and anything else you need."

When they arrived at the house, there was nothing left. Just ashes where once there had been their little house in the country. Their dream had turned into a nightmare. It had become a pyre for a boy he'd come to love. What had happened in

the past three hours to change the way he thought about everything? He felt as though his mind was in about the same shape
as the remains of the house.

Linda Young volunteered to pick up Linda from the hospital,
where she was signing papers, and drive them to Toronto.

In the parking lot, as they were about to pull away from
the hospital, they heard someone calling Linda.

"Mrs. Hawkins, Mrs. Hawkins, I've got something for
you." They saw a nurse running up to the car. She was holding
something in her hand. Linda got out to meet her.

She gave Joey's watch to Linda. "We took it off him," she
said, "and I felt you might want it." Linda looked at the watch
she had only recently given Joey, of which he had been so
proud. The glass had melted into the frame. It was black. The
band had shards of skin hanging from it, and there was blood
on the inside of the strap. She wept. If he goes, she thought,
at least I'll have something to remember him by. She had a
vision of Joey standing in the living room of their home, steal-
ing glances at his watch and adjusting his uniform sleeve to
show it off. She heard Mike's voice behind her.

"Linda, we'd better get going." She took the nurse's hand
and thanked her, then got in the car, holding the watch close
to her, as she would do many times in the next year.

"Joey," she cried. "Joey, please don't die."

They had almost forgotten about Danny. Danny was with
Wilma and Rick, neighbors Mike and Linda had gotten to
know fairly well over the past year, but not well enough to
know how generously they would respond in a time of tragedy.
Mike and Linda were grateful for small blessings.

Linda Young drove to Wilma and Rick's house. Linda got

out of the car and gave Danny a hug. She was thankful he was alive and unhurt. She wondered if he would ever understand. She wished he didn't have to. "Danny, I've got to go and help Joey. You be good and be strong for Joey until we get back. Soon we'll be back together, and we'll all be happy again."

Danny was confused and crying. "I wanna come, Mom. Is Joey gonna be all right? Kelly died, Mom. He's gone. What's gonna happen to Joey? What happened? What are we gonna do about our house? You want me to do something?"

Wilma and Rick and Doug Young assured Linda they would take care of Danny. Linda wanted to take him with her, but she knew she would be spending all her time with Joey. She explained as best she could. Linda remembers heading to Toronto in Linda Young's car. She turned to wave goodbye, and there was Danny, looking hopelessly lost, standing near the smoldering ashes of a house that had destroyed his brother's body. And here she was riding away from him.

Linda Young drove along the highway past Barrie to Toronto. They were going more than seventy-five miles per hour in a fifty-five-mile-per-hour zone when an Ontario Provincial Police cruiser pulled up alongside and motioned them to pull over. Linda Young pulled over. She explained their situation quickly. Without hesitation the policeman got in his car, turned on his light and escorted them at rocket speed over the next twenty-five miles. They continued without incident until they arrived at the side doors of Toronto's Hospital for Sick Children.

Sick Kids Hospital is nestled amidst a complex of medical buildings near University Avenue and Gerrard Street in

Toronto. It is a solemn red brick building, almost a hundred years old. It is widely considered to have the best pediatric facilities in the country, and its research efforts are respected throughout the world.

Eleven years earlier, the treatment of burn patients during the initial trauma and rehabilitative phases had begun to change radically. At the new burn unit at Toronto's Hospital for Sick Children, doctors were performing pioneering work in the development of early coverage and skin-grafting techniques, post-burn treatment and reconstructive surgery. As well, the concept of interdisciplinary burn units promised to significantly extend and enhance the lives of burn victims. Dr. Joe Zuker, a brown-haired, soft-spoken plastic surgeon with a special interest in early coverage and late reconstruction of burn patients, presided over the hospital's new unit. Following the interdisciplinary team approach and utilizing the hospital's research facilities, Dr. Zuker and his colleagues had worked hard to develop the most sophisticated burn unit in the country. Dr. Zuker would be responsible for Joey's care.

You enter Sick Kids through swinging doors from University Avenue. In the corridor are long images of the Madonna and Child in stained glass. Stairs lead to the hospital waiting room. Lining the stairwell are portraits of the medical men who ushered in Toronto's foremost hospital complex.

Neither God nor the fathers of medicine offered any comfort to Linda and Mike as they raced through the waiting room to the reception desk. No one had heard of Joey Philion. "He's our son. He's been burned bad in a fire in Orillia. He's coming here by ambulance." They were sent to the burn unit on the eighth floor. They waited for what seemed like hours for the elevator, then walked hesitantly through the corridors, looking into each room as they passed. Young sick children everywhere. At the nursing station halfway down the hall they inquired again about Joey, and were ushered to the hospital's intensive care unit.

They could see a swarm of people in white coats hovering around Joey's bed. Many tubes, lines and catheters went to his body. There were monitors with flashing lights and peculiar beeping sounds; there were oscillators. Linda and Mike peered through the glass. They saw other acute care patients in the open area. Then a nurse approached and began to explain what was going on. As she talked, Linda looked for Joey. As the doctors moved around him, a path was cleared, and Linda could see him. She gasped and began to cry. "Mike, look at him." His body had swelled to twice its normal size. She thought he looked like a gigantic blister ready to burst. "Is that our son? Is that Joey?"

The nurse tried to explain. "Mrs. Hawkins, Joey's body is reacting to the burn, and because of the size and extent of the burn his whole body is swelling. One of the things we will have to do is make incisions in his side to relieve the swelling and prevent pressure building up that would constrict and damage the internal organs. I don't know if you know this," she said, looking first at Linda, then at Mike, "but the first forty-eight hours are the most critical period for burn patients."

It had only been seven hours. There were more than forty hours to go, two more days of interminable waiting. Linda and Mike looked at each other. The nurse continued talking, but Linda and Mike had lost the sound of her voice. They were watching Joey. "But his head," Linda stammered, "it's the size of a beachball. I can't even see his eyes or his nose. And he's getting bigger while I'm standing here. What happened to my son?"

In the next seven days, Linda Hawkins would learn more than she ever wanted to know about burns, and about the extraordinary medical intervention that would save her son's life.

Joey had sustained third- and fourth-degree burns to ninety-five percent of the surface of his body. Only his scalp and two strips of skin about two inches by four inches along either side of his chest remained intact. Skin is a complex organ. It protects the internal body against the outer environment. Its outer-most layer, the epidermis, is made up of multiple layers of epidermal cells, which are constantly replaced as they reach the epidermal surface. Just below this level lies the dermis, a thick, leathery sheath rich in collagen — a protein — hormones and the autonomic nerves, which allow the brain to control body water, temperature and the flow of blood. Also in the dermis are specialized nerve endings for the perception of touch, pain, heat and cold. If the epidermis is damaged so much that the dermis is exposed to the air — the outside environ-ment — the body begins to set up defense mechanisms to ward off airborne microorganisms. As long as the dermis is exposed, the body responds as if it were in a state of siege, which it is.

First-degree burns affect the outer layer of skin, the epider-mis, only. No significant functions of the dermis are affected. A first-degree burn may fester and blister, but it will heal quickly and leave no scar. An iron brushing against your hand would produce such a burn. Second-degree burns are deeper, but again no serious tissue damage is involved. Both the dermis and the epidermis are affected, but the skin and tissue will regenerate quickly with little or no scarring. Third- and fourth-degree burns damage the layers of fatty tissue that are just under the skin. Such burns destroy the dermis and penetrate to muscles, tendons and sometimes even bone. The wounded areas swell and blister grotesquely. Nerves are severed. As the swelling increases, the resulting pressure constricts the inter-nal organs. The body can't take in fluids, or expel them, so kidney failure is also a danger. The doctors who looked at Joey were also worried about his blood circulation. Lack of circula-tion leads to infection, which might kill him. If he survived the first forty-eight hours, they could more clearly assess the extent of internal damage and think about treatment. The doctors thought his chance of surviving was minimal. They weren't sure what was keeping him alive.

The doctors made the incision to relieve pressure on Joey's organs. Then they began to "debride" his entire body — they removed all the loose dead skin, which if left untreated would cause infection. Joey was given morphine to ease the pain, but his raw skin, hypersensitive even to the flow of air in the still room, was being assaulted with scrubbing brushes, cleansing ointments and scalpels. With the epidermal layer of skin removed and the internal swelling, Joey looked like a piece of bloated meat. What was left of his skin hung on him like ill-fitting, tattered rags.

It was this condition that relatives and medical staff looked upon, and spoke often of death. Many thought it better that he die right then, and said so. Many felt that, for better or worse, there was little chance that anyone in his condition was going to survive. Even Linda at times wavered. "God," she prayed, "if you're going to take him, take him now. Otherwise leave him to me and I'll take care of him."

Linda and Mike were glad they had family and friends in Toronto. But what could their family or friends say? What could they do to lessen the impact of the tragedy on their lives? Linda remained at the hospital, and rarely ate. Three days after her arrival she still wore the dirty, bloody clothes in which she had found Joey. Her friend Arlene wanted her to take a break. Linda got as far as the car, then changed her mind. She needed to be there for him. "If I left and he died I would never be able to forgive myself," Linda explains. "And each time I went into the room, I thought, well, this could be the last time, and I just couldn't deal with that."

Joey was given intravenous fluids and blood transfusions, a catheter and therapeutic drugs to control his body. He had been given morphine to control his pain. His mind, mercifully, was beginning to drift, but for the most part he remained conscious. Over the course of a week he returned gradually to his normal size, but his skin, or the eschar that remained, looked like nothing Linda had ever seen before. Joey's doctors were shocked by the extent of his injuries, both internal and external.

Throughout the first week they could say only that he was on the edge, hovering between life and death. He was disoriented. He couldn't open his eyes because of the swelling, and he could not speak. Linda encouraged him to communicate by moving a corner of his swollen lips, once for yes, no movement for no. She would stand by his head and tell him what was going on. She became his eyes and ears, his anchor and link to this world.

Linda's mother and father, her sisters and brothers, other relatives and friends visited as much as possible. Andy Philion, Joey's father, visited; Mike was there. Many of Joey's visitors thought he was not going to live.

On the fourth day, Linda was sitting downstairs in the hospital waiting room, tired, lost in thought. She might have been praying. She heard someone calling her name quietly. When she opened her eyes, a priest was standing over her. He had a kind, understanding face, and she responded immediately. She needed to talk to someone.

They sat side by side. Linda liked the soothing voice of the priest. He spoke of God and little children coming unto Him. He spoke of salvation through Christ and heavenly bodies who sang God's praises. He talked of peace that passeth understanding. But he was talking about Joey as if, as if. . . .

He had taken both her hands in his. "Linda, when God calls us from this world there is always a purpose, no matter how it seems to us at the time. We don't know why sometimes, and we don't want it, but God is merciful. He gave up His son, and now, Linda, maybe He's calling Joey to Him, and He knows how you feel because His son, too, died as his mother watched. . . ."

Linda pushed his hands away and looked into his eyes. "Why are you saying this to me? You don't know what you are saying.'' She was crying. ''Joey is not going to die!'' She got up and ran to Joey's bedside.

''Joey, they all think you are going to die. Fight, Joey. I'll fight with you. Think life, Joey. I'm thinking life, and you must, too.'' She remained with her head beside his, silent, listening to his labored breath, willing him to live because she loved him.

She fell asleep.

Mike arrived a short time later and looked in through the window at the mother and son, side by side. He saw great pain there, an immense pain, but he saw love, too. As he thought this, he saw that Linda's eyes were open. She was looking at him. He had an eerie thought that she knew what he was thinking. They both smiled, and he went in to stand beside her. He wanted to say he loved her and he loved Joey and he would be here by their side. He said, ''Danny will be here soon.'' He put his arm around her.

Linda dreaded the thought of Danny seeing Joey. Would Danny recognize his brother lying on the bed? When the swelling had been at its worst, she couldn't see the features of the face; the nose, the eyes, the mouth had looked like small, unidentifiable eruptions breaking out in familiar places. Now, at least, the body was that of a human being, and if she looked closely, she could recognize the once strong boy.

When Danny arrived she talked to him, explaining as best she could what had been happening to Joey. She took Danny to the library to show him illustrations of different types of burns. She gradually led him up to pictures of very bad burns. She explained slowly, carefully, what a burn was and what happened to a person who was burned. She felt sick.

Danny said he wanted to see Joey.

At the side of the bed Danny stood with his mouth open. He just stared. They were silent. Finally, he said, ''Hey, that's my brother. That's Joey. Hi, Joey, it's me, Danny.'' It was painful to watch Joey curl the corner of his still swollen lip in a caricature of what had been a beautiful dimpled smile. But it was a smile. He couldn't say much through his swollen lips, and he couldn't turn his head to see Danny. He indicated that he wanted to see his brother clearly. Linda lifted Danny above the bed, directly above Joey's head. Danny screamed out, and Linda put him down. She assured Joey that Danny was afraid he was going to fall, but she was convinced Danny screamed because he saw too closely the charred remains of his brother's body.

As they were leaving, Danny said, "I guess he's gonna be okay, Mom, right? When he gets out of here, I mean." Danny paused. "When's he gonna get out, Mom?"

Why did she have to remain so strong when she felt so weak? "Yeah, he's gonna be okay, Danny. But it will take a while, and I have to be with him a lot. Do you mind, Danny, if I spend a lot of time with Joey for a while? You know I love you and we'll be together soon enough, all of us — you, me, Mike and Joey — but for now I have to be close to him."

They walked out of the room. It was some time before Danny answered. Linda didn't really expect an answer. She was simply explaining what had to be done. And then Danny said, "Mom, if you weren't here, Joey wouldn't make it, would he? Like, I think he needs you, Mom. I'll be okay."

Linda picked up Joey's watch. It had become a talisman. Each time she picked it up, she could see Joey strong and proud in his cadet's uniform. It gave her strength. She was not allowed to take it into Joey's room, because of the isolation procedures, so she left it on a ledge just outside the door. She could see it through the window. It was still black, and there were still shards of skin attached to the band. She couldn't bring herself to take them off.

She went back into Joey's room. His monitor was slowing; he was showing fewer and fewer signs of life. She began whispering to him. "Joey, just a bit longer now. Hold on. They've got everything ready for you now. You just have to hang in there a little longer. Danny's still here. You were sleeping for a while, but he was so glad to see you, Joey. He's sitting outside now." She talked to him until the nurses came in to change his dressing.

She left Joey, degowned and stepped into the hallway, reaching automatically for Joey's watch. It wasn't there. Then she spied Danny fiddling with something in his hands. It was the watch. She screamed out at him without thinking. Even as it was happening, she regretted yelling at Danny. But the watch had gone through the fire with Joey. She knew it might be the last item of his she would ever hold. The fire had destroyed everything. She grabbed the watch from Danny's hands.

Danny had scratched away the dried blood, peeled off the shards of skin and removed the smoke and dirt from the facing. Linda saw a light blinking on and off. She stared at it in disbelief. Mike came over, and they both stood, staring, unable to believe the watch was working. There was a small button on the side to set the time. Mike pressed it. The time appeared, the seconds ticking away as if nothing had happened. They were astonished. Linda thought it must be a sign of some kind. She embraced Danny, who was happy that his mother's wrath had been transformed to joy. The watch became a symbolic heartbeat. As long as it was still working, Joey would live for another day.

For seven long days Joey hovered near death. Slowly his body, at first one long, open wound, began to regain a normal shape. Each day Linda gently rubbed the sleep out of Joey's eyes. By the fourth day one of them was clean enough to open. Initially Joey could see only shadows, and he thought he was blind. His mother told him his eyes would need time to focus again because they'd been closed for so long. He could barely move his lips, but he could say yes and no. The morphine cut the edge of the pain, but it left his mind wandering. Nobody, not even Joey, knows where his hallucinations took him. But the pain was great, and often he was brought back forcefully to the searing agony of consciousness.

Joey's sanitized hospital room wasn't much of a world. There were stainless-steel trays, endless white bandages and rolls of gauze, saline solution, bottles of blood, poles and lights and plastic tubes attached to monitors that lit up and made strange noises. Into this room they came, one after the other; green-coated and white-coated doctors, nurses and technicians and orderlies. Joey would close his eyes when he saw them coming; he opened his eyes only when he knew his mother or Mike was there.

Often the monitors showed Joey's vital signs ebbing, and each time Linda's presence in the room would stop the descent. It became a topic of conversation among the nurses. "He's weakening," they would say. "Call his mother."

Linda spoke with the doctors. One in particular she liked. He was honest and informative. He would tell her what state Joey was in, and his rate of progress. There was never much to report in the way of progress. It was a miracle to everyone that Joey was hanging on.

The doctor told her there was still the possibility of brain damage and blindness. If he's blind, Linda thought, he'll not be able to stand living. That would be too much for him. And if he was brain damaged, if the doctor was indicating that he was going to be a vegetable, what was the point of keeping him alive? She thought that if necessary she would put him out of his misery herself if it turned out to be true, but on both counts she felt the doctor was wrong. She had already rubbed the sediment out of Joey's eyes and knew that he could see shadows. As for his brain, well, they were simply wrong. She had asked Joey if he remembered what happened and he had said yes. She asked Joey if he remembered their dog. She didn't tell him that Kelly, the dog, had died in the fire. He remembered Kelly. She then asked about the cat. Joey looked puzzled. "No cat," he said, his swollen eyes and lips looking grotesquely bewildered. And he was right. Linda was simply testing his memory and orientation. And to her it was clear, even if it wasn't to the doctors, that his brain was fine.

But what if he died anyway, just as everyone was saying he would? That was the most terrifying thought. If he dies, she said to herself, then I'll go with him. She didn't know what death would bring, but he was in such pain, he had gone through so much and he was so young she couldn't imagine him going alone into the unknown. The thought stayed with her throughout the first critical days, and she was terrified of it.

Linda also met Dr. Clark, a young plastic surgeon who worked under Dr. Zuker in the burn unit. He had never seen anyone as badly burned as Joey. Dr. Clark told Linda the team had decided that Joey's chances for survival would be far greater if he were transferred immediately to the Shriners Burn Institute, Boston Unit, one of the most renowned burn institutes in the world. He explained in detail the reasons for the transfer. The Hospital for Sick Children at one time had the technology to graft skin cultures, and they still did it in some cases. But their technology was limited. If Joey were to survive, he needed to have his body covered quickly with new skin. The Shriners Institute would cover Joey's body with artificially cultivated skin while they tried to set up a way to use what little was left of Joey's own skin for a graft. The doctor explained that it takes about three weeks for a skin culture to grow, and Joey needed about ninety-five percent new skin. They were looking at months of extensive surgery and post-operative care. Boston was equipped to handle such extensive surgery. Toronto was not.

Linda adamantly refused the transfer. She wanted to be close to friends and family. What would she do alone in Boston? How would she cope with months of painful operations? She wanted to discuss it with Mike, but he was driving Danny back to Orillia. She knew Mike had to remain in Orillia to help Danny and to work. He could get down to Toronto nearly every day from Orillia, but how would he get to Boston?

Dr. Clark pressed her to reconsider. If she wanted Joey to live, she had no alternative. "Linda, your son will die if he stays here. I can't even assure you that he'll live with the treatment he gets there, but I can assure you that it is his only chance. If you want to give him that chance, sign these papers and we'll have him transferred in the morning. Shriners has already agreed to the transfer."

Linda reluctantly signed the papers, then went upstairs to explain to Joey what they were going to do. She stayed with him for a long time. Her thoughts drifted to the past. The future existed only in terms of the next few minutes, the next hour, the next task. And the tasks were becoming more difficult.

She was afraid Joey wasn't well enough to make the trip. She would have to be with him. She told the doctors she wanted to be on the plane with him. Initially the doctors refused, but Linda was insistent. She returned to Joey's bedside to await their decision. He was afraid and asked her not to leave him. She explained that the doctor was going to get back to her, but she would do everything she could to be on the plane.

"Joey, look at me and listen." She was looking into his eyes. "If they say there is no room, I'll look at the plane myself to make sure. If they say it's against policy, I'll beg them to change the policy. If there is any way possible, Joey, I'll be there. And if not . . . well, we'll deal with that possibility later. But for now, Joey, you have to understand that no matter what happens I'll be with you. Do you understand? I'll be here."

He was struggling to answer. He tried to move his arm but

became frustrated when unable to do so. She tried to make out what he was struggling so hard to say.

"Home. Mom, I want to go home. Please take me home."

"Joey, you can't yet. But we'll be there soon. First we have to go to this place in Boston and they'll fix you up, and then we'll all be going home, okay? Joey, you have to understand. You're hurt bad. It will be a while before we go home. Try not to struggle right now. You need all the energy you have for the flight."

While she and Joey waited anxiously for the doctor's answer, Mike arrived at the hospital. Linda had left a message with Doug and Linda Young asking him to return to the hospital. His face was white, his hands shaking. They all waited. The doctors finally agreed to let Linda go on the air ambulance.

She ran to tell Joey the good news, but he was surrounded by nurses and doctors preparing him for the trip, and they would not let her in immediately. "He has to know that I'm going with him. I have to tell him," she pleaded. But there was too much going on. She asked a nurse to give Joey the message. When she was able to see Joey, she told him she was going.

"I know," he said, and smiled.

The next morning, after last-minute arrangements and tearful goodbyes to relatives, Linda got on board the air ambulance. Mike and Andy would meet them in Boston. Linda thought it ironic that Joey's lifelong desire to fly should end up being realized like this. She explained to Joey everything that was going on around him, how high they would be flying, their speed and expected time of arrival. He had always loved the details of flying, and she told him as much as she knew before takeoff.

The trip to Boston was a nightmare. Joey was weak when they started out, and he was becoming weaker. His blood pressure and vital signs continued to drop; the pain increased.

Drops of blood and green discharge were seeping through his bandages. He alternated between shivering with cold and being feverish. He was becoming systemically infected.

The nurse accompanying Joey didn't want Linda near him during the flight. She was nervous. It would interfere with her routines, she said, and she thought it was unsafe. Linda tried to sit unobtrusively in the background. She heard the doctor ask for the rest of the morphine. The nurse replied that they had used all she had brought.

Finally, Linda undid her seat belt, moved up beside Joey and began talking to him quietly. The nurse grabbed her arm and told her to return to her seat, but the doctor noted Joey responding, and signaled to the nurse that it was okay. Linda stayed by Joey's side for the rest of the trip. She was hanging onto a hope that was as faint as the beating of his heart.

CHAPTER THREE

They arrived in Boston late in the afternoon. An ambulance was waiting at the airport to transfer them to the Shriners Institute, where they were met by an army of nurses and doctors dressed in the hospital's trademark blue scrubs. Joey was wheeled to a bacteria-free, sterile room to be assessed. Dr. Susan Briggs, Shriners' assistant chief of staff and a plastic surgeon, took one look at Joey and booked an operation immediately.

He was weak, close to death. The doctors weren't sure Joey would live through an operation, but they were sure that if they didn't operate he would be dead before morning. They needed to debride him again immediately; then they would assess the course of medical treatment.

As he was being wheeled away, Linda began crying hysterically and running after him. A nurse was explaining the procedure to her, but the explanation seemed confusing. Mike hadn't arrived yet, and Joey was out of sight. Linda felt lost.

Pat Cartigainer, the institute's social worker, found Linda chasing after the stretcher. She introduced herself, put her arm around Linda and said, "Linda, let them help your son." Linda allowed herself to be led to a chair. She sat and cried quietly. She told Pat she was drained and upset after the flight, and that she wanted to see Mike. She talked to Pat for two hours. Then Pat went to the operating room to see if she could get a progress report. They were still in the initial phases, the doctors said. They would have to remove the remaining eschar and dead tissue as quickly as possible — excising, they called it — otherwise systemic breakdown could result. Joey was showing few vital signs. He might not make it through the operation.

Linda wanted to share Joey's pain, and she wanted him to know that she was there with him. She became quiet, looking inward, seeking him in a prayer.

A team of nurses and doctors swarmed over Joey's anesthetized body, which was bathed in the light of the overhead lamps and in topical chemotherapeutic agents. The doctors peeled away layer after layer of charred dead skin. Blood seeped from Joey's body. Transfusion tubes replaced his blood, and the monitors registered his stable but weak vital signs.

Outside the room Linda was feeling faint. She tried intensely to enter her son's mind, to stay there with him. She heard herself repeating from some place deep within her, life, life, life. All around her, the antiseptic smell of death permeated the halls.

The first operation at Shriners Burn Institute took ten hours. His body had once again swelled to twice its normal size, as it had during his worst moments back in Toronto.

When it was over, Linda was given more consent forms to sign. Things were happening too fast. She tried to read the papers through her tears. She noted that one was a consent form allowing the doctors to amputate his feet. She was horrified. The doctors explained that Joey needed all the energy he could muster for the other parts of his body. His feet were beyond saving. They were burned clean through to the bone. Linda thought they were going to take her son apart piece by piece.

She felt vulnerable and powerless. She was assured that most of the papers she was being asked to sign would authorize routine procedures. Joey risked serious infection, and other complications could arise if they had to wait for consent at any point in his treatment. The consent forms were a precaution, they explained.

If Linda had been uncertain about Boston before, she was far more worried now. Maybe we can get him sent back to Toronto, she thought. She wanted to talk to Mike.

In time Linda would come to regard Shriners Burn Institute as most of the world did — as the most advanced institute of its kind. The children who come to Shriners are the victims of burns, chemical spills, explosions and house fires that leave their young bodies beyond the reach of traditional medicine. Shriners Burn Institutes across North America pioneered and advanced the use of early skin-grafting techniques. Their doctors use natural mammalian products, such as skin from human cadavers, to cover a patient's wounds while they wait for the patient's own skin to grow and cover the injury. They have made advances in surgical techniques, anesthesiology and the use of blood banks. They have developed potent antibiotics to ward off infections.

Children come to Shriners institutes from war-torn El Salvador, from the Middle East, from Asia. They are sent from Canada and from all over the United States. Their medical expenses are underwritten by the Shriners, a vast organization that has listed among its members John Wayne, Ronald Reagan and Red Skelton.

Linda rarely met a Shriner in person, though she saw many

of them with their telltale red hats — fezzes — walking the halls. They asked nothing of her. Occasionally they offered her words of support. She knew that Shriners had underwritten the millions of dollars it would cost the institute to save her son's life. That was a priceless gift.

Shriners Burn Institute is not a place for the faint of heart. The institute is situated directly across the street from Massachusetts General, at the center of a massive hospital and research complex in downtown Boston. Just off of Cambridge Street and facing Blossom Avenue, Shriners is easy to overlook. When you climb the winding steps and walk across the red brick patio that graces the entranceway, you enter another world. A large, cheery-looking waiting room with stuffed toys and a television is filled with children waiting to see their doctors, and adults waiting for their children to come from one of the institute's three units. There are approximately thirty beds in the three-floor hospital, which is usually filled to capacity. Tears and anguish mark the lives of those whose children enter Shriners' wards. Families go through emotional upheaval — anger, pain, confusion, fear, guilt and a sense of utter vulnerability.

The staff of the institute have developed a profound sensitivity to the parents and children who come for treatment. Their philosophy is grounded in the recognition of the whole person: "Every child admitted to the Shriners Burn Institute is an extremely valuable and important person and deserving of the best care possible. His worth as an individual is of paramount importance, and all aspects of care must take into consideration the child as a whole person with individual needs. The hospital recognizes that children are not 'little adults' and therefore strives to provide an environment which focuses on the special needs of the patients as children or adolescents. The child is, in addition, an integral member of the family unit, and every effort is made to support this relationship, to provide the informational and special needs of parents and to assist parents with their responsibilities to their child.'' For many of the children who come here, Shriners is a last resort. Like Joey, they require extensive surgery and reconstruction that many less specialized hospitals can't provide.

Massachusetts General Hospital, the teaching and research facility with which Shriners is affiliated, and Saint Francis Hospital, in Hartford, Connecticut, provide a steady supply of residents who wish to specialize in burn treatment. They are obvious to even the most casual observer in their operating-room blue scrubs. They stay for two-month rotations at Shriners, working in its restricted second-floor labs, with research animals, or in the bacteria-controlled environments where human and artificial skin are cultivated. Residents are on call twenty-four hours a day, and they assist in operations under the direction of Dr. Briggs, assistant chief of staff, and Dr. J. Remensyder, chief of staff. The residents give a sense of ongoing research and medical solidity to Shriners.

The daily round of work of Shriners nurses is more like a vocation than a job. Parents beg, plead and bargain with the nurse, as if the nurse were responsible for their child's condition.

The nurses assume a pseudoparental role over children whose bodies are burned beyond recognition. At the end of each bed a nurse's chart, their bible, outlines the course of treatment they are to follow. Routinely, they look upon and tend to children in severe pain. They become familiar with the language of pain and the role of medicine in restoring life to young bodies. Nurses at Shriners are noted for pushing children hard, much harder than they want to be pushed, in order to regain optimum use of their bodies, once they have started to recover. Some of the children complain, and some profoundly dislike their nurses. Some bond closely with the nurses; they become

closer to the nurses than to their own parents. Some of the
children die.

It is the nurse who breaks the news of death. It is the nurse
who shares in the daily toll of tragedy. And it is the nurse who
is blamed by parents for the course of treatment the children
undergo. Parents hold the nurse responsible because there is
no one else as close to their children. In the parents' minds,
the nurse is the guardian of medical mysteries.

Linda Hawkins knew nothing about hospitals or institutes.
She had not had much need of them before the accident. She
had traveled to an unknown city far away from family and
friends only because the doctors in Toronto had said she must.
The doctors in Boston had scrubbed the long, open wound
that Joey's body had become. They had removed all the dead
tissue. They were considering amputating his feet. Joey's body
was once again swollen and bleeding from the scrubbing. For
eight days she had been on a death watch. She wanted to sleep.
She wanted to cry. She wanted to wake up from her nightmare.

Mercifully, Joey was sleeping as she sat at the foot of his bed.
Joey was in Bed One, the bed reserved for the most critically
ill patient. The unit was an open area, so Linda could see the
comings and goings of everyone in it. She could see the flicker-
ing lights of the monitors over the beds. She watched as nurses
and doctors huddled at the foot of a child's bed. She watched
as nurses attended to her son and to the other children. She
could hear children crying. But she heard laughter, too. She
couldn't remember the last time she had heard laughter, but
she liked the sound. Perhaps one day she and Joey would laugh
again, she thought. But for now she could only look at her
son. He was spread-eagled on the bed, covered with bandages

from head to foot. He looked like a crucified mummy. From the bed she heard the occasional low, mournful wail, signaling Joey's return to consciousness. It would be a long time before they would be laughing, she thought.

Mike and Andy were late getting to the hospital. They were having trouble persuading customs officials to let them across the border. Mike had lost all his identification in the fire, and Andy hadn't thought to bring his with him in the rush to leave Toronto. Customs officials kept them for hours despite their pleas and explanations. A letter from Toronto's Hospital for Sick Children explaining Joey's condition did nothing to speed matters along.

"Who's the father of this boy," the customs official asked.

"He is," Mike said, pointing at Andy, "but his mother is my wife."

The official looked puzzled. "His mother," he said, pointing at Andy, "is your wife?"

"No, no, Joey's mother is my wife. He's the ex."

"So why are you both going down?"

"Because they need us."

"Both of you? Why doesn't one of you go down? How is the mother going to handle both of you?"

"I don't think you understand," Mike explained. "We've got to get over there, now." But he himself wondered momentarily how Linda was going to handle both of them. It couldn't be said that they were the best of friends any more and, although tragedy had brought them together, it hadn't necessarily changed the quality of their relationship. But this was only a momentary thought. Joey needed Andy. Linda and Joey needed Mike. And these officials were complicating matters unnecessarily. The customs officer finally phoned Shriners and agreed to let Mike cross. Andy was detained for another four hours.

Mike was furious. When he and Andy had decided to fly

to Boston, Joey's condition had been extremely critical. What if he died, Mike thought, startling himself with the realization that death was a possibility, perhaps as inevitable as the approaching weekend.

When Mike arrived, Linda explained what the doctors wanted to do. "Mike, they want to cut off his feet. They say they're beyond recovery and a source of infection. They want me to sign the papers, but I wouldn't. What are we going to do?" She was frantic now, unleashing all the anger and fear and frustration she'd been sitting on while waiting for Mike, waiting for Joey to open his eyes.

"Linda, calm down. We'll talk to the doctors. We'll find out why. We'll find out what's going on and then we'll be able to make a decision. Can we go up and see Joey first, though?"

They did, but Mike stayed only a short while. He looked at Joey, looked at the child victims surrounding him, felt on his increasingly clammy skin the cloying smell of burned flesh and death, and walked outside and was sick.

It was late the next day before Linda, Mike and Andy met with Dr. Briggs and discussed Joey's treatment. The doctor explained that they would use artificial skin, which was cultivated on the premises, to cover and protect his body from bacterial microorganisms and from hypothermia. Then they would gradually cover him with autografts of his own skin, which they would take from his scalp and chest. If he were lucky and all the skin grafts were accepted by his body, Joey could be covered with his own skin within six months, and he would then be out of danger. Until then, he would be prone to urinary-tract infection, respiratory infection, vascular infection, loss of blood, hypothermia, various fevers, pneumonia and a host of other life-threatening diseases. The human body, Dr. Briggs explained, could only withstand so many operations before it would weaken and finally die. The doctors didn't know yet what Joey's tolerance level was. He would need a lot of support to go through the pain. She was surprised that his body had been able to withstand as much as it had already, but she could offer no guarantee about the future.

Linda took to the sandy-haired, articulate woman immediately. Dr. Briggs was open, honest and very knowledgeable, and she exuded understanding. She explained everything they needed to know as best she could, and she told them to expect everyone to be open with them throughout their stay. Linda thought Dr. Briggs was the kind of person she could trust to care for her son.

How long they were going to stay, Dr. Briggs explained, depended, of course, on Joey. If he had survived this long, then there was a slight chance, maybe ten percent, that he would get through, but again, she wasn't about to guarantee that. Recovery was a long and painful process. Even as they were speaking, Joey was being prepared for another life-saving operation, to debride him, to remove any remaining dead tissue and to take a skin graft. The feet could wait, she said, but the toes would have to go soon. They hadn't survived the fire, and Joey needed his strength for the rest of his body.

It wasn't good news, but it was honest. Linda began to feel that at least she understood what was going on. She and Mike and Andy agreed, reluctantly, to the amputation, and they thought that if Shriners could work on Joey's body, they themselves could work on his will. Together they could bring him back to life.

In the next two weeks, the boundaries of the family's world assumed a definite and bleak reality. Linda and Mike moved into Halcyon House, a support house where the parents of Shriners children could stay for twenty dollars a day. There they met other parents whose children were suffering, other people who were in an unknown city, confronting unexpected tragedy. They spoke in different languages, but their common plight bonded them to one another.

Neither Linda nor Mike wanted to talk, and everyone there

understood and left them alone. It was comforting in some
way to be quietly understood, not looked at with pity or consoled by people who were unable to understand or appreciate
the depths of their emotional confusion and turmoil. Halcyon
House became a refuge. It was a place where Linda and Mike
would learn to laugh again.

Every day, Mike and Linda walked along Charles Street,
through the Boston Common and the Public Gardens Park,
then through Beacon Hill or along Cambridge Street to
Blossom Avenue, and climbed the steps to Shriners. It was
March, and the coastal city was often gray and overcast, driz-
zling rather than raining. The city mirrored their life: gray,
clouded, oppressive.

For most of us, the experience of pain, emotional or physical,
is minuscule in relation to what Joey and his mother underwent. It boggles the mind to think that someone would willfully
live through such pain. To imagine what Joey's body looked
like, think of a piece of steak. Think of your arms and legs,
your thighs and buttocks, your back and your feet and hands
resembling this piece of meat. Think for a moment of that same
red meat going bad, turning brown, then gray, then green.
Think of the smells associated with rotten meat. Think of a
human body looking like this, and swelling to twice its size.
This is what Joey's body looked like.

The task of the Shriners Institute was to heal this dysfunc-
tioning mass of flesh and blood through cleansing with
medicinal ointments, which would ward off infections, and
debriding with scalpels, to prepare it for skin-graft operations,
a process Shriners pioneered and continues to refine.

There is a mind animating the body. In Joey's case, the mind
was medicated with elephantine doses of morphine and
methadone and other sedatives. Somewhere within this wrecked
and weakened body, which had shrunk from a hundred and
thirty to eighty pounds in less than three weeks, was Joey

Philion, thinking, hallucinating, suffering excruciating pain that even the morphine could not touch.

We do not know what he was thinking or seeing. He mercifully forgets, although he remembers scenes from the period, and some conversations he can repeat verbatim. At times, his mother and other visitors thought he was unconscious. At other times, Linda would watch with horror as his eyes registered the intensity of his desperation and terror. With the white gauze bandages almost completely covering him, all she could see were his eyes. She and Mike and Andy say that what they saw there they will never forget.

When Joey first entered the hospital Dr. Briggs considered him to be in a life-threatening condition. They had to remove the dead tissue from the burned surface completely. They did this by shaving the skin with a scalpel, peeling back layer after layer of charred or waxy white layers of subcutaneous tissue. Then they scrubbed until the wound was open, cleansed and granular — or ready to accept a graft. Joey's body swelled and bled profusely after each such operation.

From the initial operation and assessment, a nursing plan was drawn up. Joey was given head-to-toe dressing changes twice a day. Each change took about two hours, because the bandages were eight layers thick. During the dressing change, nurses would look for signs of sepsis or infection. They would find sources of infection by the smell and color of the discharge oozing out of Joey's body. Topical cleansing agents, including bleach, would coat and cleanse the skin, and the bandages would shield it from airbound infection. Often hydrotherapy is a staple of a burn victim's treatment. But too many factors made hydrotherapy dangerous for Joey. Hydrotherapy is contraindicated for newly grafted patients until ten days after grafting, hemodynamically unstable patients, patients with biologic dressings that are adherent to the wounds, patients receiving paralyzing drugs, or anyone with a base temperature of ninety-eight degrees. Joey's condition included all these contraindicators, and more.

But bedside debridement could not be sustained continuously; tub baths became an essential therapeutic feature of his regimen, and bleach was added to the water. An open wound exposed to the air is excruciatingly painful. To touch it is worse. To place it in water is worse still. Add bleach to the water and the pain becomes unthinkable.

Since Joey's body was so weak, most physical functions were performed or stimulated artificially. An intubation tube attached to a respirator and channeled through his nose regulated his breathing. Suction tubes were channeled through his mouth. Catheter and intravenous lines were everywhere, monitoring urine and channeling blood and other necessary fluids. Sedatives and antibiotics were pumped in regularly.

Joey was placed in strict isolation. Everyone who saw him was required to wear gloves and masks and gowns, and anything that touched him was sterilized. Heart, pulse, blood and temperature readings were taken through the monitors. Sputum, blood and urine samples were taken daily. If a monitor registered a change, a corresponding change was made in the tubes entering or leaving his body. For much of the time Joey was encased in a plastic, bacteria- and temperature-controlled tentlike unit just beyond the front doors of the open ward. Without this maze of medical intervention and technology he would have died. And despite all of it, not even the most expert doctors know why he lived.

His face, which had been grotesquely burned in the fire, regained its original plasticity and look. After each operation, his body and face would swell up. They resisted removing the skin from his face. But for his scalp and two thin strips on his chest, Joey's skin was virtually destroyed. The skin from these "donor sites," as the undamaged chest and scalp area were called, had to be peeled away, stretched, artificially cultured and regrafted to his body.

Joey underwent forty-one skin-graft operations at Shriners. On average he was operated on once every three days. For each operation, his primary nurse came to his bedside and removed the bandages from the area of his body the doctors would be working on. Then the area was cleansed with sterilizing ointments and lightly scrubbed. It was wide open, without protective covering, red and raw, overly sensitive to touch and even to the flow of air. The nurse covered the area with two layers of light gauze wrap. The donor sites were shaved or scrubbed to prevent infection. Then Joey's lips were moistened with petrolatum, and his eyes were cleansed with saline-soaked cotton. The nurse looked for signs of conjunctivitis or drying of the cornea. Exposed tendons, muscle and bone were cleansed with a diluted soapy solution and kept wet at all times. Then the nurse documented on a flow chart the status of specific regional burns. The nurse described wound appearance, and clinical signs of infection such as change of color, cellulitis, malodor or purulent exudate. The nurse noted the care administered and any special needs of the patient. A resident ascertained Joey's preoperative condition. Then the nurse called the orderlies to take Joey to the operating room.

The orderlies placed Joey on a special stretcher and wheeled him through the front doors of the unit, past the gray elevators and straight through the double doors of the operating room. Then they moved him onto the specially designed operating table. Two large saucerlike lamps shone down onto the table. Dr. Briggs or Dr. Remensyder or a specialist conducted the operation, and a varying number of blue-coated, white-capped residents were on hand to assist. There were also nurses to assist with the procedures. The doctor removed the gauze, then examined the sterile area, looking for the granular appearance that indicated it was ready to accept an autograft.

A Dermatone or Dermabrader is a machine that looks and operates much like a carpenter's plane. It was used to shave off a paper-thin outer layer of one or two inches of skin from

Joey's donor sites. That skin was then placed in a cultivator, where it was stretched, perforated and prepared for the graft. The prepared skin looked like a thick piece of fishnet stocking.

Joey was anesthetized. The skin that was to be used in the graft was taken from a sterile tray. It was placed over the sterile raw area with forceps and tweezers. Then it was stapled onto Joey's body with a staple gun and a staple about an eighth of an inch deep.

It took about fourteen days for the donor site to heal, and three weeks for the graft to become part of the living organism of the body. (Even years later, the grafted piece of skin will retain the fishnet appearance.)

During his operations, Joey was unconscious, under a general anesthetic. Joey used to beg for the operations. Only then was he free of pain. It didn't matter that he would wake up to new pain. He wanted only to be out of his misery.

After each operation, the physiotherapist moved Joey's body through a series of exercises designed to mobilize his stiffened joints. Because he was anesthetized, the physiotherapist could move his arms and legs without causing him any pain. Doctors assessed his body.

After the physiotherapy, the orderlies pushed Joey back through the operating room's swinging doors, back past the elevators, in through the green doors that marked the entrance to the unit. Joey slept until the daily round of pain began again, to be broken only by the next operation.

Between operations, nurses checked the graft area daily. If the graft was accepted by the body, the skin remained healthy-looking and began to attach itself to the body, to become a living part of the organism. A certain percentage of the grafts were not accepted. They became infected and had to be removed to prevent further contamination.

During dressing changes, the nurse looked for discharges in or under the graft area. She smelled the site and noted the color. The nurse could identify the source of infection and respond accordingly. If the graft was accepted by the body, the nurse need only keep it clean. If it was not accepted by the body, she could cleanse the area with extra ointments, including bleach, to kill the bacteria, then do extra dressing changes and check for sensitive pressure points impacting on the graft area. All pressure must be uniform. If these postgraft interventions are successful, a potentially unsuccessful graft can be restored with minimal loss. Parts of the graft that don't take in a given area will gradually join up with the other parts that did by growing and stretching out toward them until the entire area is covered. Medical intervention at this point consists of enabling the body to heal itself.

Joey's body was in a postoperative, medically controlled state — swollen, bleeding, suppurating and prone to numerous infectional diseases — for more than seven months. He was in constant pain. He was given powerful muscle sedatives, which would paralyze him for a week at a time. He could not open his eyes, could not speak, could not move a muscle. But he could still feel the pain, since even morphine could barely take the edge off it.

Twice a day or more his dressings would be changed. The dressing changes caused pain all along his wounded body. His wounds were extremely sensitive to touch. To place a finger on any part of his body caused pain, but the dressing changes involved constant grasping and pushing. He, his nurses and his mother had to steel themselves for the ordeal twice a day.

Joey's joints grew stiff and painful, and all movement became uncomfortable. Wanting to avoid the discomfort caused by moving, Joey tried to close his body in on itself, to immobilize it. His physiotherapist, Kelly, had to stretch and push his body. Joey equated Kelly with the torturous regime that, ultimately, would restore movement to his limbs. He would plead with Kelly to stop — but silently, because he couldn't make a sound with the intubation tube cutting off his vocal chords. Joey believed Kelly when she said the therapy was necessary if he wanted to regain his mobility. Even through the pain and the fear, he was looking ahead to the day he would be well again. The few muscles he had left in his upper arms, hips and upper legs were exercised to regain their strength. These muscles often went into severe spasms, a problem that plagues him still at the time of writing.

During the months of recovery, the nerves in Joey's body, many of which had been destroyed in the fire, were regenerating. Raw, tingling nerve endings, hundreds, perhaps thousands of them, screamed out in pain each time Joey's body moved, like a thousand toothaches erupting simultaneously throughout the body. When the skin regrafted successfully, the staples had to be removed with a pair of tongs. Each graft took numerous staples. Each staple had to be pulled out.

Finally, every day, Joey's chest was pounded, to prevent the fluid building up in his lungs. Each day, as Joey edged closer to life and away from death, he had to suffer an unending cycle of agony. Life itself became a continuum of physical and mental horror.

For a few months, Joey could not move his neck. His eyes, disturbed by the swelling, the pain and the morphine, were focused on the ceiling above him. For months, he lay fully bandaged with only his eyes exposed. It was with his eyes that he expressed himself.

Joey's nurses and visitors became intimately familiar with his eyes. They pleaded, showed hopelessness, looked lost, screamed, shed tears, laughed and loved. Many times his mother watched as the light in his eyes diminished. Other times, Linda was terrified for him, but it was life those horror-filled eyes were communicating. It was the "death eyes," as she came to call them, that frightened her the most.

For months no sound came from Joey, not even a sigh. The

intubation tube went straight down through his vocal chords, cutting off all form of utterance. For five months Linda communicated with him by asking questions and letting him blink his eyes in a coded answer.

Joey was not alone. Surrounding him in the open unit were other children in several states of recovery. Joey came to know them by the sound of their screams. He would mark time by the regularity of their routines. He would worry if he did not hear a particular child's mournful voice, because that meant perhaps the child had died.

Joey remembers waking up many times and listening to the agonizing screams of a child. They would get louder and louder, until suddenly it dawned on him that it was he, Joey, who was screaming, and that he was hearing a sound no one else could hear.

On March 19, little more than a week after the fire, Joey had undergone three operations to debride him, to take skin from his donor sites and to cover his body with artificial skin. Without the operations he would have died.

Dr. Briggs told Mike and Linda that every operation was life-threatening. She anticipated that, if everything went well, it would take at least six months for Joey's body to be covered. It would take twice as long with complications. Until his body was covered with skin, Joey's condition would remain critical. Linda resolved that she would remain strong. She willed her body not to get sick, to withstand the sleepless nights she spent by his bedside. Medical technology would take care of Joey's body; she would take care of his heart and mind.

On March 20, Mike had to leave to return to his job in Orillia. Linda and Andy stayed. Andy was having a hard time. He couldn't bear to see Joey in so much pain, but he stayed with his son many nights. He knew Joey wanted him there.

None of them was prepared for the kind of suffering they were witnessing. Everyone was suffering, not just Joey. It was a jarring, sobering way of life. According to Jeff Foley, a spokesman for the Shriners Institute, Joey was the most critically burned child they had cared for in their twenty-year history. Joey stretched their knowledge to the limits. Dr. Bradley, a large, intense and informative resident who treated Joey during the initial phases of his stay at Shriners, told Linda that Joey's courage and tenacity inspired him to be the best doctor he could possibly be. "We have the resources here to aid Joey and we have to use all of them to the best of our ability if he is going to survive," Dr. Bradley said. "Even then we may not be able to do enough. But it won't be because we aren't trying as hard as anything we have ever attempted in our lives."

Joey hallucinated constantly. He could say nothing, because of the tube in his nose, but he showed with his eyes that he was frightened by the hallucinations. Linda stayed by his bedside and slept at the hospital. During the early stages he would wake up and look for her. He would call out for her, telling her with his eyes of the frightening visions he was having. He would focus on her face, a face that sometimes seemed distorted due to the hallucinatory quality of his vision, but he would find an anchor and she would soothe him with her eyes, with words of comfort. Gradually he would calm down and drift back into a fitful sleep. Linda resolved to remain on call twenty-four hours a day, seven days a week, until Joey recovered. She asked the nurses to call for her if Joey needed her.

On March 23, Linda's birthday, she recorded in her diary that Joey wished her a happy birthday and that she responded that it was the best one she ever had because she got to spend it with him. She meant it. She had been told countless times by friends, relatives and medical staff that he was going to die any minute. But he had survived. She wasn't sure where he gathered the will to live with unbearable pain in a body burned beyond recognition. She knew only that he was comforted by her presence.

On March 28, Joey and Linda spoke about the fire. It wasn't the first time, but it was the most extensive. Joey communicated by blinking his eyes and mouthing phrases, which Linda interpreted. He remembered everything. He remembered yelling loud enough to wake Danny, then running through the wall of flames in the living room to her room, only to discover that she had gone. He remembered racing back through the blaze to his room and the hope of escape. They both cried. He said he would do it again if he thought his mother and brother were in danger.

And he told her again that he wanted to go home. He didn't plead this time, as he had in Toronto. He told Linda that he had to go home for her sake and for Danny's. "When we get home, Mom, everything will be okay again," he mouthed. "Don't worry. I'm going to be okay." He asked her if she and Danny were okay. Once assured, he fell asleep.

On April 1, the doctors informed Linda that they wanted to take more of Joey's feet. Linda was afraid he would lose his will to live if they removed too much of him. If it was necessary, they could do it, but how and when would she tell Joey? He didn't know he had lost his toes. Linda was afraid of what the knowledge would do to him. She knew the best way to deal with the situation was to tell Joey everything as honestly and clearly as she could. But now she hesitated. She knew she would have to tell him soon, just as she would have to tell him that Kelly had died in the fire.

On April 3 Joey asked how the fire had started. Linda told him she felt she must have left a log smoldering in the wood stove. He was silent. Then they both wept.

Later that day, after she had left, she wept uncontrollably for hours.

For the first few weeks, Joey was easily infected. Each time the nurses changed him, each time the doctors operated, he was prone to any bacteria in the air. His body interpreted the skin grafts as a foreign body and rejected them; infection set in. The doctors covered his wounds with artificial skin as much and as early as possible. But his body rejected the artificial skin. The resulting infections caused hypothermia and fevers.

In addition, the loss of blood from the operations necessitated constant transfusions. Joey received about five pints after each operation. Occasionally Shriners ran out of his blood type, and would have to put in a radio request for donations. Blood donors were hard to find, given the fear surrounding blood transfusions and AIDS-related diseases. Sometimes the doctors used another closely related type of which they had an abundance. Joey's body was being covered with new skin, and his blood was replenished with an entirely different strain. Joey was living in another body.

On April 4 the doctors performed another operation. They put steel prongs in his fingers to stop them from bending permanently. His hands, like his feet, had been burned right down to the bone. There were no remaining tendons, so recovery would be limited. The prongs would limit the extent of the damage and aid in the cosmetic aspects of recovery.

By April 10, one month after the fire, Joey remained in extremely critical condition. Doctors Briggs and Bradley couldn't understand what was keeping him alive.

When the nurses changed his bandages, Linda would study Joey's body. In most areas she could see through the thin membrane that sheathed his internal organs. There were holes, large gaping holes in his thighs where his muscles used to be. The nurses were filling them with gauze. His arms were only an inch thick; so were his legs. She looked at his feet. The doctors had talked the day before of amputating Joey's leg below the knee. They felt the risk of infection would be reduced significantly. Joey's kneecap had dissolved in the fire. The doctors weren't sure if he would regain mobility in the leg. Joey complained about it constantly. He had pneumonia and fluid in his lungs. His vital signs were weakening; his blood gases were low. Dr. Bradley had come down during the night

to speak with Linda. The doctors had decided to paralyze Joey
with Pavulon, a powerful sedative. It would stabilize his condition but not improve it. They were simply prolonging his
life, Dr. Bradley said, and he couldn't guarantee that Joey
would live through the weekend.

Linda waited, clutching Joey's watch in her hand. It was
still working.

Joey didn't die that weekend. Dr. Bradley told Linda he had
never seen anything like it in his life. Joey shouldn't have been
able to live even if he were just lying in his bed. But here he
was having a major operation every two or three days, and
he was surviving. The doctor couldn't understand it. He was
becoming optimistic in spite of his knowledge. Something
remarkable was happening.

By the middle of April, the media had picked up on the story
and sent it around the world. Numerous journalists went from
Ontario to Boston to record Joey's progress. Fund-raising
events were taking place in Orillia, Joey's hometown, and
people from across Canada were sending in donations and letters of support. The president of Mattel toys sent Joey a huge
plastic white and black eagle. Joey had it set above his bed
so he could always see it. Perhaps in his mind he could ride
away on it.

Mike phoned, as he did every night, to check in on Joey
and to offer his support. Linda, as always, pleaded with him
to come to Boston. Both Mike and Linda knew it would be
difficult for Mike to stop work and leave Danny to spend all
his time in Boston. But Linda needed him as much as Joey
needed her.

Finances were a constant problem. Neither Mike nor Linda
had money. Before the fire they were barely making ends meet;
what little they had was wiped out in the fire. A trust fund
established in their name in Orillia helped to defray some of
their costs, but the financial difficulties remained.

The trust fund board members would give Mike travel

expenses, but it was clear they wanted him in Orillia, fulfilling what they saw as his duties, namely, rebuilding and providing for his family. The fund was growing by thousands of dollars daily, through donations and fund-raising events. The Orillia *Packet and Times* crusaded for Joey's cause; it published a daily report on his progress and asked for letters of support, especially letters from young people. Mike knew Joey enjoyed the letters; they seemed to strengthen his will.

Mike wanted to stay in Boston. He knew he wouldn't have a family if Joey died. He scraped together some money and returned to Boston in mid-April.

By this time the media had spread the story of the courageous boy who refused to give up. Hundreds of letters and gifts were arriving daily for Joey. Many Canadian newspapers were encouraging their readers to send letters of support, and the readers responded with unprecedented generosity. Each day, Boston postal workers brought two large bags of mail for Joey. Linda read him the letters and he was cheered by the thoughts of people, some thousands of miles away, who were thinking of him, encouraging him with their thoughts and their prayers. At first she wasn't sure he even heard her. (Joey told her later that he drifted in and out of consciousness listening to the sound of her voice, hearing the words, forgetting his pain. He remembered some letters almost word for word and repeated them months later.) At first, it was Linda who was made stronger by the show of support; later the letters helped to strengthen Joey's resolve to live.

On April 16, Joey began calling out for Wayne, his young friend from Orillia. No one could understand what he was trying to say, not even Linda. She asked him questions to which he responded with the eye code. She finally understood that he wanted to see his best friend.

Linda called Wayne's father in Orillia and told him Joey was close to death and wanted to see Wayne. The next morning

Wayne was on a plane to Boston. Joey was paralyzed at this time. The only time he could communicate was between doses of the paralyzing drug, Pavulon. Linda had learned to ask him questions about his condition or wants during the period when the drug wore off and the new dose had not yet taken effect. He would be conscious for minutes before the next dose sent him back to unconsciousness. Neither his inability to talk nor his fluctuating level of consciousness appeared to disturb Wayne.

Wayne was a fresh breath of Canadian air in the sterile hospital environment. He was wearing pastel shorts, a brilliant red shirt, green running shoes, sunglasses and a visor with a layer of colored lights that blinked across his forehead. He bounced through the hospital listening to music on his Sony Walkman.

Mike and Linda described to him the dismal world he was about to enter. They introduced him to Joey's nurse, then took him to Joey's bed. Joey was fully covered in bandages, and paralyzed by drugs. Wayne was shocked at first. He sat on the edge of the bed for a few minutes, staring at his best friend in silence. "Joey," he said "Joey, it's me, Wayne. I'm here."

No response.

"Joey, this is one hell of a way to get out of school. I would have chosen something different myself, like driving in through the front doors of the school on our bike. . . . But then, it probably would have broken down before it got through. Hey, Joey, you should see the bike now. I mean, it is awesome. I got the brakes on, and the clutch only slips now and then, not like before. You got to see it, Joey. Hey, Joey, I couldn't believe it when I heard about it, the fire, I mean. I went there with my father. We saw the trucks coming and followed them. It was just awful, Joey. Do you remember me at the hospital? Hey, listen, did you hear about. . . ."

And so the monologue went. For nine days, Wayne Cooke

Jr. sat at Joey's bedside, telling bad jokes, updating Joey on the cadet squadron's developments, passing on condolences. Wayne articulated the dreams their friendship was based upon, and demonstrated that their friendship was still alive despite the fire and the pain and the distance that separated Joey from the life he once shared with Wayne. Joey slipped in and out of consciousness. Occasionally he would attempt to mumble something or look into Wayne's eyes. (Months later, Joey repeated portions of Wayne's bedside monologue to his mother and told her how much Wayne's presence had meant to him at the time.)

When he wasn't talking to Joey, Wayne talked to other patients and ran errands for the nurses. By the end of Wayne's visit, Joey's vital signs were stronger than they had been for weeks. Wayne left reluctantly, but happy that he had helped his friend through a critical period.

On April 28, Danny arrived. He was elated to be seeing his mother and brother again. Linda tried to spend some time with him alone. They walked along Rowes Wharf and sat on the benches in the Public Gardens and fed the squirrels. They talked about Joey and about what Danny had been doing. And they spent time in the hospital. Joey was happy to see his brother. He wanted to be assured that Danny was okay, that he wasn't burned. They listened to music Danny had brought.

On one of their visits Joey wanted Danny to give him a hug. Danny was reluctant. He had just seen Joey's nurse checking his lines and tubes and had watched and listened to his brother's painful response. Linda had explained that Joey was sensitive to touch. Danny didn't want to hurt Joey, and politely refused to hug him.

Linda, Joey and Danny spent time together at the hospital. Joey began to feel stronger, and one day he asked for a mirror. He had not seen his face since the accident. Linda got him a mirror. She had been adamant about not letting the doctors remove the skin from his face. The swelling had gone down significantly, and Joey's face, not ravaged by the fire, looked like a gaunter version of his old face.

She watched his eyes as he stared into the mirror. Linda could see that he looked relieved. He had expected much worse. He said he was happy his face was fine, but he knew what the rest of his body was like. He wondered what it would be like when they returned home. Mike and Danny returned to Orillia the next day. It was always difficult on the last night. Linda knew Mike had to go back, and Mike knew she didn't want him to. They avoided the conversation, but it hung over them like a shadow. Linda spent most of the time giving Danny much-needed attention, something he seemed to need more of as the months of separation continued.

On May 6, Dr. Jo Buysky, an enthusiastic new resident, told Linda that Joey was going to be moved to a private room, to protect him from potential infections. Linda checked the room. It was small, but it had a TV, and she knew Joey would like that. Joey fell asleep watching the TV. (This was a good sign: pain often kept him awake.) Linda left to get some rest. He had just awakened when she returned, and he wanted to watch TV again. While they were watching one of his favorite programs, Joey began to choke. Linda triggered the alarm bell connected to the nursing station next door. She didn't know what to do, and she waited agonizing minutes for the nurses. She couldn't understand what was keeping them. She thought perhaps her sense of time was off, due to her panic. Finally she ran out to the nursing station. No one had heard the alarm. Linda and a nurse ran back to the room. Joey's face was beet red, his eyes bulging. Within minutes the nurse had everything under control.

Linda, meanwhile, was convinced that Joey's new room was unsafe. She lived every day with the possibility of Joey dying, but she was not going to lose him because of a failed alarm system. The nurse agreed that the room was unsafe, and assured Linda they would have the alarm repaired by morning. Linda didn't want to leave him there overnight. The nurse assured her they would be checking on Joey constantly, but Linda was adamant. She would not move from the room until something was done. An hour later Dr. Buysky informed Linda that they were moving Joey back to the floor. He would be placed in a "bacteria-controlled nursing unit" — a plastic tent with air and temperature controls — because his body was still vulnerable to infectious microorganisms.

The nursing unit was safe, but it prevented Linda from sitting close to Joey. She walked around the unit, then tried to fit herself inside it. A nurse politely but firmly indicated that that undermined its purpose. Linda knew she was right, but she still didn't like it. Joey didn't like it, either. The head nurse had given permission for Linda to enter once a day, but it was hot inside and Joey wasn't happy about the heat and the isolation. However, he accepted it more willingly than his mother. "They've got to protect me and the other kids, so I guess it's okay for a while. The quicker I get better, the quicker we can get out of here." Linda marveled quietly at his inner strength and the maturity he showed. She didn't know at that point that the pain and suffering were going to get worse, and that both of them would be even more severely tested in the upcoming months.

Joey was depressed, disoriented and afraid. He continued to mouth responses to his mother's queries. He told her about his hallucinations. He said he saw people in the room, people he knew. They were sitting on his legs, or pulling on them. He would yell at them to stop. He also tried to describe to Linda a disturbing and oppressive dream. He was never quite able to explain, and Linda tried to help him forget. She would talk to him until the morphine- and pain-induced images receded.

Joey was suffering from sleep deprivation. All he wanted to do was sleep, but sleep would come only in snatches. Long stretches of sleeplessness gradually increased to eight, ten and fourteen hours. Consciousness was unending agony. And, as the inability to sleep continued, the agony along with the drugs left him confused and disoriented. The only person he really knew was his mother, and even she was sometimes lost to him for brief periods.

Linda was getting two hours of sleep a day. She slept at the hospital — on couches, in the waiting room, in the basement, anywhere where there was a cot, a bed or a chair. Many nights she found herself alone in the hospital's chapel, a tiny room with a meditative landscape painting on one wall. She could smoke in the chapel. Within the silence of that small room, she felt alone, cut off from everything. One night, after a visit to the chapel, she returned to Joey's room feeling very afraid of death. Joey was fighting off a massive infection, and he had pneumonia again. His vital signs were weak. The doctors once again predicted death. They didn't think he could withstand another bout of pneumonia.

Linda went to the side of his bed, still praying, still questioning. She spoke softly to him. "Joey, if you go, if you want to go now, or if you can't fight it any longer, I'll go with you, Joey. I'll go because I don't want you to go alone, and I don't want you to have to put up with any more pain. It would mean I would have to leave Danny and Mike." She was crying. "I want you to stay with us, Joey, but if you want to go I won't let you go alone."

She had many such private conversations. She never told anyone about them, not even Mike. She wasn't sure if they meant anything to Joey. (Much later, Joey told his nurse what Linda had said to him that night, and how it had moved him to fight just one more time.)

After two months, Linda was tiring. The pain was getting

worse, and neither she nor Joey could take any more. It was the same every day. Joey would wake up and call out for Linda. The nurses would find her, and she would sit by his bed, talking, calling his name, soothing him with her voice. He would beg her to stop the pain. Sometimes he forgot where he was. Gradually she would calm him down and help him return to peaceful sleep. Doctors Remensyder and Briggs decided Joey's body was too weak to withstand any more operations. In mid-June, he was once again sedated with Pavulon, sending him into a week-long state of what amounted to suspended animation.

They suggested that Linda go home.

Both Joey and Linda needed a rest.

CHAPTER FOUR

In Orillia, Mike was trying to do what he sensed was required of him. He was working at the factory, thinking of the future and of rebuilding the family's shattered life. The fire had wiped out everything. There was no house and nearly no Joey. Mike was living in a cottage near the old house. It had no running water, no electricity. It was cold and small and lonely.

Mike also had to contend with the media. Reporters had turned a private nightmare into a public drama, and now Joey and Linda and Mike had to live up to some public image. But Mike wasn't sure what was expected of him. He was nervous whenever he had to talk to reporters. Jeff Day, editor of the Orillia *Packet and Times*, had remained supportive and sensitive in his coverage of the tragedy. As the people of Orillia rallied around the family, Day kept a running coverage of Joey's progress. He announced upcoming fund-raising events and tributes. As a result, the trust fund, which was administered by a group of professionals whose life experiences were about as different from Mike's and Linda's as they could be, grew enormously. The money would pay for Joey's medical expenses and the family's immediate needs. But dealing with the trust fund was not easy for Mike.

The only time Mike felt comfortable with the situation was when he flew to Boston to be with Linda and Joey. There were no questions then. He was the loving companion, the emotional supporter and father — roles he accepted willingly. Then he would return to Orillia, and try to live the role that others were foisting on him. Provider and future-builder. He became bewildered. Who was he supposed to be providing for? What future lay ahead? Boston was clearly where he belonged. But where would he get the money, and what would people think?

Vulcan Hart Industries, the factory where Mike worked, was supportive. They gave him time off to go to Boston. His co-workers would ask him about Joey and Linda and he would explain, but somehow the words were not enough. He had been down there. The reality of what he saw was etched into his mind, but the pain he'd seen and the agony he felt were beyond his skill to talk about. And who would want to hear about them? And what part would they understand?

"He's really not doing great, but he's hanging on. He's a fighter," he'd say. And the men and women around him would nod and offer words of sympathy and advice; he appreciated the tenderness with which they sought to understand and console him. But they hadn't seen Joey's body. They hadn't waited, not once but daily, for the death doctors predicted was just around the corner. They hadn't seen the desperate pleading in Joey's eyes or received Linda's equally desperate late-night calls. They hadn't felt the fear that knotted in Mike's belly. They hadn't seen Linda.

And then, of course, there was Danny. He knew he was supposed to remain strong for Danny. But they were living in a damp, cold cottage with no running water. It was hard to be the father he felt he should be. Danny was difficult to handle at the best of times; during this tragedy, he was impossible.

And Mike's guilt was as sharp as a knife. He would contemplate what might have been, and contrast it with sobering reality. Were it not for the furnace and the cold and the house and the constant struggle to make ends meet, Joey might be fine today. Mike became depressed.

Linda had heard as much from neighbors. When he discussed it with her she urged that "no matter what anyone says, we are not going to blame each other. That will destroy us both and that won't help Joey. We just have to accept that this has happened and deal with Joey as he is now . . . together. Don't let anything or anyone else distract you, Mike. I know it's hard, but we have to be strong. Joey and I both need you."

Boston was clearly where he belonged. The hospital would take care of Joey's body, Linda would take care of his mind, and Mike would take care of Linda.

The original trust fund started small and mushroomed beyond anyone's expectations. It began at Joey's school, among classmates and teachers. As it grew, the school principal went to the Huronia Trust Company, in Orillia, and they established a fund to which many people could donate. It was called the Hawkins Family Trust Fund, and the money would be used for Linda, Mike and Danny to reestablish themselves. No one thought Joey was going to make it.

It was not always clear when Linda or Mike could use the money in the fund. Should they build a house, buy clothes, fly to Boston, feed themselves? They needed money desperately, but after a few encounters with the people who took care of the public fund, Linda and Mike wondered about the whole enterprise.

Both Mike's and Linda's signatures were required for every check, along with information about where the money was going. But Linda was in Boston and Mike was in Orillia. It was hard to get the two signatures. Linda received money for her rent at Halcyon House — twenty dollars a day — and ten dollars a day for incidental expenses.

Mike knew that building a house was the family's most important task. With a house, the family had a future. Mike could bring Danny home, and he could work to pay off the debts he had accumulated before the fire. Most important, Linda and Joey would have a place to come home to.

Mike went out after work to look for a suitable site upon which to build. He and Linda felt uneasy about moving back to Cleveland Avenue, the site of the fire. How would Joey feel? It didn't seem right.

Trust fund board members, however, thought it perfect. No cost for a new lot — they could just build. A new house, just what they needed. Finally, Mike agreed.

For two months, June and July, board members kept putting off the start date for the new building. They gave Mike no clear reason. Then a company called Colonial Homes approached Mike to say they wanted to build a home for Joey. They were willing to build at cost — about fourteen thousand for the shell and ten thousand for the fixtures. They would get suppliers to go in at cost, too, and the Lion's Club would help. Mike was overjoyed.

Mike phoned Linda, and Linda called the board members. They agreed that such a project was precisely what the fund was for, and they encouraged her to go ahead. There was about eighty thousand dollars in the fund at this time.

Linda and Mike were thankful for the generous way people had responded to their tragedy. They knew the money in the trust fund had come from all over North America. But having to deal with the bureaucracy that administered the fund was sometimes difficult — for the trust administrators as well as for Mike and Linda. Board members were ultimately responsible for determining whether a particular expenditure requested by the Hawkinses was necessary, and the decision making was not always easy. Often particular decisions became tangled in personal, legal and medical questions.

In the end, the house became lost amidst the legal and medical wrangling. The trust fund board members announced that the board thought fund money should be used solely for medical expenses; the house could not be seen as a medical expense.

In the spring, Linda had taken a trip to Orillia, and Linda and Mike spent their first night alone together since the fire. They had only a few short hours to share the love that until a few months before had remained untested. They discovered, unexpectedly, that their feelings for each other had deepened. It was Mike's birthday, and Linda had bought him a ring, a symbol of their relationship. She had wanted to give him something precious and expensive, to show him how much she cared for him and needed him, but she couldn't afford to be extravagant, so she bought the ring. Mike was touched. He and Linda learned that a bond had formed between them in the wake of their tragedy, a bond stronger than either of them had known. They talked about Joey, about the fire, about their feelings, which they were powerless to explain to others. For a little while, walking along the banks of Lake Couchiching late in the evening, listening to the water lap against the shore, they could be just two people in love, walking hand in hand, enjoying a warm night.

It was a brief respite. Linda returned to Boston the following morning.

Linda sat at Joey's bedside reading.

> Dear Joey:
> We have been following your progress in the papers. You are a brave boy Joey. You are probably hurting right now, but you'll get better Joey. Think of being home again with your mom and your little brother and your dad. It won't be long Joey. We will think of you every day until you get out and do many more brave things with your family.

The hand-drawn card was signed by more than sixty children from a school in western Canada. Joey had received thousands of letters, cards and gifts from people of all ages and from many different places. Linda felt honored to be reading the cards to a boy the world thought of as a hero. She marveled at the courage he showed during the long, lonely nights at Shriners. She was happy there were thousands of people rooting for him, wanting to comfort and support him.

She was aware of the pain and suffering of the other children and their parents here on this unit of mercy and sorrow. Two children had already died. One of them had suffered second and third-degree burns to thirty percent of her body after lighting herself on fire in a suicide attempt. Ultimately, she succeeded. Without the will to live, this young girl, weak and unable or unwilling to stand the pain, had died during the third week. Others were severely burned, their bodies scarred beyond recognition in parts; their minds, like her son's, were filled with suffering. Some of the lucky ones were waiting to go home. Joey wasn't waiting to go home. He was waiting for death to pass by.

Linda spent hours talking to other parents and relatives. She had watched, helpless, as parents collapsed under the relentless onslaught of the brutal world their children were reluctantly confronting.

I'm lucky, she thought. Many, many people were supporting Joey. She could see it and hear it in the number of letters she was getting.

Why Joey? She was unable to answer this.

It was impossible for the Canadian public, especially those closest to Joey in his hometown, to ignore the real-life drama that was unfolding in Boston. They sang the praises of a young boy who almost died in a valiant effort to save his mother. His mother in turn suffered with him by his bedside. It was unselfconsciously heroic, and people were dramatically moved.

Love for his mother drove him into the fire, and the love of his mother kept him fighting with all his strength to survive. As Joey continued to fight tenaciously against such overwhelming daily pain, many were moved to struggle with him. They wanted to participate, and to inspire him with their dreams as he had inspired them.

Mike would tell Linda of the Ontario reports and occasionally someone would bring down a pile of articles for her to read. More frequently she met with the parade of print and broadcast journalists who would regularly visit and record his progress. She would read the reports speaking of Joey as "the little Canadian boy." She wasn't sure about the media. Joey wasn't a little Canadian boy, or a hero, or anything other than a physically devastated boy. She felt she had an obligation to keep the press informed, but often the press unwittingly interfered with the bedside vigil. And anything that interfered with that risked Joey's life. Frequently, disheveled, having just spent a harrowing night outside the operating room, or watching Joey fighting off another medical assault, she did not want to encounter the press. But if any one thing motivated her to inform the public through the media, it was a young and innocent girl framing love songs and enchanting pictures of the outside world for Joey hundreds of miles away.

Linda knew Nia Herhily only through her letters to Joey. She wrote from a small town near Barrie, Ontario. Nia had first heard about Joey on the six o'clock news. The network had showed a picture of Joey before the fire, and Nia saw him as a happy, smiling, strong young boy. Then there was the fire that destroyed his strapping young body. It was unfair. It wasn't right. Nia was moved. She cried for two hours, and for days afterward she found herself crying whenever she thought of Joey. She wished she could take his pain away.

She didn't know why she was moved so intensely. For days she tried to understand her emotions. She wanted to do something for him, stop the pain, bring him back to life, encourage him, even hold him if she could, but he was far away, and she didn't know him. So what could she do? And why did she need so much to do it?

Nia kept informed of Joey's progress by reading the papers and watching the evening news on television.

As the weeks went by, Nia began composing a letter. She told Joey who she was. She described herself and some of her interests. She told him that he was a remarkable young boy, and that she was supporting him, willing him to live. She explained she was not someone who wrote to celebrities. (By this time Joey had attained celebrity status.) She didn't know why, she said, but she knew she was bonded to him, and she would stay with him throughout his ordeal. He must fight to live. It took her some time to compose her letter. The letter paper and the envelope were light blue, and decorated with stars and pictures of animals and palm trees and little jokes and surprises. Then she wondered if she should send it. Would he understand? Would his mother understand? In the end, Nia mailed the letter. And she resolved to write every week, to tell Joey of life outside the hospital. She would tell him about her friends and family, and describe the feelings in her heart. She would tell him what any young girl would tell any young boy who was brave: that his struggle was worth it.

Their relationship had begun.

Her parents, both teachers, found her concern touching. Her father, an avid outdoorsman and naturalist, had taught Nia to appreciate nature. Her mother's Celtic background had inspired Nia's love of music and poetry. The love in the family had given her a generous heart.

Linda smiled as she picked the letter up from the pile that arrived that day. Her second sense told her before she opened it that it was special.

"Joey, this one is from someone named Nia. It's got a cow standing on a beach, and a beachball. There's an ocean in the background. There are cows with sunglasses on." Linda found these images funny in a quirky kind of way. The letter, too, was interesting, and when she finished reading, she thought about the world's many compassionate people. She set Nia's letter aside in a special place. A week later, another letter arrived from Nia. Linda could tell it was from Nia by the color of the paper and by the little cows with sunglasses. She smiled and began reading. Nia described a day in her life. She spoke of the seasons, the work she did, school and young boys, her father and mother, her sister, the music she enjoyed. She asked after Joey, and encouraged him to remain strong and to dream of going home. She sent him her love.

When Linda stopped reading Joey looked up and asked if that was the same girl who wrote before. Linda indicated that it was. "And what's her name again," he asked, mouthing the words with difficulty around his respiration tube. "Nia," she said. Nia had said she loved him. They both smiled.

Nia was not thinking her letters would be regarded as special. She had told her parents she was writing every week. She wanted to help Joey, she said. She thought Joey deserved to live after heroically rushing into a fire, saving his brother and almost dying trying to save his mother.

It her fourth or fifth letter to Joey, Nia told the story of the phoenix rising.

The letter paper was green, blue and yellow, with pictures of a grinning Tyrannosaurus Rex clothed in a flashy Florida-style beach outfit. Butterflies climbed along the side of the page. The story was dedicated to Joey, "the real phoenix."

The Phoenix

The Phoenix was born on a mountain.
Out of fire and ashes.
As it had from the beginning of time
   the beautiful bird of purple and gold
   spread its wings out forever and arose in flight.
Each day the Phoenix would rise to new heights
   discovering the deepest secrets of the earth.
It grew in wisdom each day,
   forever uncovering the hidden virtues of life.
One day the Phoenix grew weary.
It knew that it was time.
It headed for the mountain.
The Phoenix drew near to its birthing place,
   now a funeral pyre.
It lay down and burst into flame.
The pyre burned for an eternity
   until there was nothing left but ashes.

The ashes lay cold and lifeless.
There was nothing left of the beautiful bird
  that had once risen above the mountains.
Then they began to stir.
The ashes swirled round and round,
  twisting faster and faster.
Suddenly, they burst into flames
  and another even more beautiful bird
  was lifted out of the ashes.
But this Phoenix was different.
It did not fly, it soared.
It didn't rise above the mountains
  but above the earth.
And this Phoenix did not grow weary
  because when it came time to lie down,
  it soared high into the sky,
  up to the stars,
  refusing to believe that it was time to give up.
That pyre has been empty for thousands of years now,
  and that Phoenix is still flying.

So when you feel weak, Joey,
  and you think you can't stand the pain any longer,
  just look to the stars.
The Phoenix will be there.
Maybe you can't see him, but he's there.
As he once rose from the flames, so will you
And he's waiting for you to soar with him.

The letter was signed, "Love, Nia." Joey asked his mother
to read it again.
   Linda read it many times. Was there really such a bird?
Where did the legend come from? Joey loved birds and planes,
anything that soared through the sky. Linda wanted the legend
to be true. She needed to hear that Joey would rise again, even
if it was only in a poem.

Much later she would learn that the myth came from the Sumerians and Egyptians. It was repeated in many different cultures, one of a cycle of death-and-rebirth mystery stories told and retold throughout the ages. The original myth tells, as Nia did, of a miraculous bird that by an act of its own will destroys itself in a fire in its own home and then recreates itself out of the ashes. The bird returns to its home, which has also risen up out of the ashes, and, like the bird itself, the house is transformed.

For many cultures the eagle, soaring free above the earth, combines with fire in this way to create a profound image of transformation. The self dies in order to find wisdom. Other myths in this cycle replace the bird with a young man who goes through a period of suffering, often near death for a time. But he returns to his people transformed, bringing with him visions of the hidden inner world.

Linda stared at the eagle hanging from a wire above Joey's bed. She told Joey to think of it as the phoenix. And she wondered how a mythic tale could so perfectly intersect with real life.

Joey loved Nia's poem. In her weekly letters, Nia would remind Joey to recall the phoenix when he was in pain. She would tell him to soar and to rise again.

Nia's letters were special to Joey and his mother. Among the thousands of gifts and words of encouragement, the letters of this young girl with the name of an ancient princess touched them both.

Much later, Linda received a visit from *Toronto Star* reporter Jim Wilkes. Among other more pressing concerns, she mentioned Nia's letters. He was touched. Returning to Toronto, he asked his editors for permission to try and locate her. He drove to a small town near Barrie, Ontario, following the postmark on the envelope, and asked at a corner store if anyone knew a girl named Nia. He explained that he was writing a story and wanted to meet her. The woman behind the counter happily directed Wilkes to Nia's home.

He knocked at the door and Nia herself answered. He explained who he was and why he was there. Would she be the Nia who was writing to Joey Philion? Staring at him in disbelief, she told him she was. Within three months she would be meeting Joey face to face, but now the happy recognition that Joey Philion was responding to her overjoyed Nia.

Nia's place in Joey Philion's struggle would receive wide recognition. Her picture would appear in numerous papers and her poem would be shared with hundreds of thousands of *Toronto Star* readers. Life for this shy and pretty seventeen-year-old would never be the same again. And Linda and Joey were delighted with this unexpected show of caring.

Nia wanted neither praise nor recognition. In this she represented the tens and eventually hundreds of thousands in North America who were responding to an event that staggered their collective imagination. Joey's struggle had inspired such widely conflicting groups and individuals as the president of Satan's Choice outlaw biker clan, the prime minister of Canada, Buckingham Palace — The Queen's Printer sent a letter of sympathy and support — sports heroes like Larry Bird, Bobby Orr and Wayne Gretzky, air and armed forces bases across North America, youth groups and police associations. It was Joey's ability to inspire widespread generosity of spirit that gave hope to what was otherwise a meaningless tragedy.

Joey's struggle continued with monotonous regularity.

CHAPTER FIVE

Boston was hot in the summer. When Linda went to Halcyon House to sleep, the room was baking.

She began to have bad dreams. First she dreamed that her father died, then that Mike died. Then she had terrible dreams about the fire. After such dreams, Linda would go to the hospital early, thinking how perverse it was that she appreciated the air-conditioned hospital, despite its suffering, more than the comfort of the street or of Halcyon House.

Joey was still disoriented much of the time. The doctors were worried about infections establishing themselves in his nose and throat. Recent skin grafts were not taking, which meant more time in hospital, more open wounds, more operations, more pain.

Joey still could not talk, because of the tubes in his nose and mouth. He begged the doctors to remove them. He wanted to talk to his mother and Mike and to the nurses. The residents worried that he might lose his ability to talk if the tubes remained in much longer; they might damage his vocal chords. In this condition, depressed and weak, Joey passed his fifteenth birthday, on June 4, 1988. All through June Joey's blood pressure was high. His doctors worried that he might have a stroke, and they checked his blood gases every few hours. Finally they decided the tube could come out at the end of the month if Joey's breathing remained stable. It was the best news the family had had in months.

Linda informed Joey of the decision and encouraged him to keep fighting. Joey knew that, with solid food and conversation, he would quickly regain strength and be able to go home sooner. His psychological and physical condition began to improve dramatically. He began to fantasize about the kinds of food he'd be able to eat. Finally his doctors realized that he was starving.

Linda thought the respiration tube that kept him breathing also kept him chained to his bed. The monitors surrounding his bed could not be wheeled around with him, and each time a machine was removed from his body, Linda was happier. She thought he might be able to sit up soon, maybe even go outside in a wheelchair. He had not seen the sky for four months. In Linda's mind, sitting up was just one step away from going home. She and Mike waited anxiously, and Joey began counting the days.

Mike had returned to Boston with Linda after her short visit to Orillia. He began to look for work in Boston, to help defray their costs. He was slowly fitting into the routine the hospital imposed on them. Each day he and Linda would take care of Joey, talk to him for hours, help with therapy or dressing changes. Half of Joey's body was now covered with new grafts, and Mike and Linda could observe the appearance of the healed skin and imagine what the boy would look like when all the grafts were done. They also encouraged him to move his arms. Kelly, Joey's physiotherapist, said this would help to prevent contracture of the skin. If the skin became too tightened, an operation would be required during the rehabilitative stages to regain the freedom of movement constricted by the contracture.

Joey was not easily persuaded. Every aspect of his life involved pain, which he endured stoically. But to impose the pain on himself by moving his arms was too much. He did it very reluctantly for the nurses; he didn't want to do it for his protectors, as he came to view Linda and Mike.

One evening Mike was returning from a walk through the winding, cobblestoned streets of Beacon Hill. He passed a priest about a block from Shriners. Mike found himself turning around and standing in the middle of the sidewalk, hoping the priest would talk to him. Mike wasn't usually one to talk to priests, or to anyone in authority, for that matter. The priest was young, Mike thought as he observed him closely, perhaps not even twenty. He wasn't threatening, and he didn't come across like a priest. He held out his hand and said, "I'm Father Michael."

"I'm Mike. How about I'll call you son and you can call me father," Mike suggested. "That way we won't get confused." They both laughed, then began walking along Blossom Avenue. Before long Mike found himself telling this comforting stranger about everything that had happened in the past few months. They sat and talked for an hour. Mike took to the priest immediately, and he thought Father Michael liked him, too. Mike invited Father Michael to meet Linda, and they set up a date.

Father Michael was comfortable and engaging. He listened with understanding and compassion. He cared about people, and he didn't preach. They wanted him to meet Joey. He said he would be honored.

Father Michael had never been to Shriners before, but he had been through many different hospitals, and they were all the same. They housed the crippled and the lame and the suffering. As he walked down the ward he noticed the three-foot-high poster of a voluptuous brunette in a red bikini at the foot of Joey's bed. The figure was headless. Nurses and friends would rest their heads on the cutout section and pose for Joey.

"Joey," Father Michael said, laughing, "My bishop has asked me to come down and make sure you are not watching dirty movies." Joey's eyes widened, and he grinned, embarrassed.

Joey communed with Father Michael as his parents had. Often the priest would come by the hospital late at night. He had an uncanny habit of showing up on particularly bad nights; for instance, when an infection had sent Joey into a fever. Joey, Mike, Linda and Father Michael would wait out the night together.

When Mike had to return to Orillia, Father Michael kept Linda company. He told Linda he felt a peace emanating from Joey, despite the pain and the hallucinations. And when Linda had to be away, Father Michael offered to take her place. He would sit by Joey's bed every day. He read letters to him and comforted him. He cleansed and massaged his wounded body, and spoke to him during long, hot summer evenings.

One June 29, doctors informed the family that Joey seemed to be breathing well enough to have the respirator removed within a week. Linda rushed to tell Joey. But that night his blood gases came back, showing that his blood was not getting enough oxygen. The doctors increased his respirations to twelve a minute. Joey had tired himself by trying to breathe independently. It seemed certain the tube would have to stay in. Linda didn't have the heart to tell Joey. It was all he had looked forward to the entire month.

Linda wanted to talk to Dr. Briggs about the tube. That meant calling her office, finding out her appointment schedule and waiting in one of the places Dr. Briggs was bound to pass in her travels from one appointment to another. Dr. Briggs was always accessible, just busy, and Linda was always asking questions. She would run along beside the doctor as she made her way between Massachussets General Hospital, just across the street, and Shriners, her home base. In fifteen minutes Dr. Briggs would answer all Linda's questions or tell her where to turn for an answer.

The next day, Linda tracked Dr. Briggs down and they discussed the tube. Dr. Briggs persuaded Linda that the respirator was a necessity. The doctors would have to play it by ear, as they had done with many things.

On July 5, the removal date was put off for one week. Joey's blood gases had improved due to the respirator, but they wanted to make sure he was sufficiently prepared before removing the tube completely. Joey was heartbroken. He knew the longer the tube was in, the more likely his vocal chords would be damaged. And, more than anything, he wanted to eat. "If it doesn't come out soon, I'll never get better, Mom. I'll just lie here." Linda tried to explain, then she massaged his face gently with vitamin E and asked him to think of home. Joey remained quiet, staring up at the great eagle that hung above his bed. Linda thought he had fallen asleep.

"Mom?"

She turned toward him, watching his lips as he mouthed a question.

"What happened after the fire? What have they done to me here?"

She told him that many times he had almost died. Although he remembered many things, there was much, mercifully, his mind had buried.

Joey told her again that it was important that they get home. It was too much for both of them, he said, to be in the hospital. At home he would be able to fight harder. "We've got to get out of here, Mom. I don't know how much more I can take."

The next day Joey wanted to sleep until the tube came out. The physiotherapy had become more intense in anticipation of the tube being removed, because with the tube out Joey would be able to sit up. But his legs were causing him almost unbearable pain. The nurses asked Linda to help with the physiotherapy, and she did. Joey managed to sleep the better part of the week, in anticipation of the tube coming out. He would wake up, ask what day it was, then return to sleep. It was an act of will.

One evening, after Linda left, a baby came in with burns to seventy percent of its body. The parents were frantic. The child died during the night. Joey, alone in his bed and disoriented, hearing the commotion, thought that all the patients were going to die, that everyone was in trouble. No one was aware of the paranoia that filled him with terror that night.

In the morning, although the ward had returned to its normal routine, he was still afraid when Linda returned. He was lying, eyes open, teeth clenched. "Mom, you're here. Tell me what happened. I'm scared, Mom. We almost all died last night." Linda didn't understand. After talking with the nurses and finding out what happened during the night, she explained as best she could, telling him that the baby, not yet a year old, had died. Everyone else was fine, she assured him. Joey cried. There was so much pain and sadness to deal with, Linda thought. They talked for hours about the baby and the unfairness of it all. That afternoon a blind retarded boy was admitted to the ward. He had crawled into a bathtub and turned the hot water on, scalding seventy percent of his body. He died within the week.

On July 20, at 8:00 AM, the doctors decided to take Joey off the respirator. They thought he was strong enough to continue the struggle on his own. At 8:15, Joey was smiling from ear to ear — a "Joey smile," as the nurses referred to it, the

smile that glowed with glory. Linda, too, was laughing. She
had forgotten what her son looked like without the tube.

For the first four hours, everything went smoothly. Then
the monitors indicated that Joey's labored breathing was not
good enough. A monitor reading of one hundred indicated that
his breathing was deep enough to oxygenate his blood. A
reading of less than ninety meant his breathing was too shallow
to oxygenate the blood. The monitor hovered around ninety-
five, just barely enough to sustain him. Linda pressed him to
concentrate on his breathing, and the scale on the monitor
would climb back to a hundred. Then, as Joey became tired
or fell asleep, it would start falling. Each time it reached ninety-
seven Linda would wake him and encourage him to breathe.
Four times it went down to ninety-two, and four times they
worked it back up again. At 5:30 AM, nearly twenty-four
hours after the tube came out, the scale was remaining steady
at one hundred. They had made it through the first day.

That afternoon Joey ate his first meal in five months. He
started with chicken soup, followed by macaroni and cheese.
Then he had a milk shake and chocolate pudding. He was
deliriously happy and wanted more. But each time he ate he
threw up. And when he threw up he was unable to eat again
for days. It was the first time he'd felt not only the absence
of pain, but actual pleasure. The tantalizing moment during
which he could taste food or feel satiated was followed by a
period of retching that led to a dry heaving cough, sending
his entire body into spasms. But so subtle and desirable was
the feeling of pleasure that he tolerated the consequences in
order to get a taste of the food as it was going down. But even
this perverse pleasure was denied him. Each time he rejected
the food, they had to rest his body for two days. It took nearly
two months for his body to learn to digest food again.

Even though he couldn't keep anything down, Joey always
wanted to eat. His nurses used his desire for food to motivate

him to get up. He didn't want to, because of the pain. It would be his first time out of bed in five months, and the unfamiliar prospect was daunting. The nurses couldn't force him. They wanted him to want to do it himself. He finally agreed to try. Linda would wait outside until he was ready.

With a nurse on either side, an orderly and a physiotherapist, they proceeded to lift him off the bed. One nurse explained the procedure and showed him the special chair that had been designed for him, which would allow him to sit in different positions.

Joey didn't want to go. They had to be careful because the underside of his body, especially his back, remained uncovered and they couldn't apply pressure there. He screamed the entire time he was being moved, and begged to be put back into bed.

But once in the chair, he was able to find a tolerable position. As the tears stopped flowing and his eyes cleared, he looked around the unit for the first time. To Joey, whose senses had been starved, the sight was a revelation. Despite his pain, a smile touched the corners of his mouth and his eyes danced. He asked Monica, his primary nurse, for his sunglasses.

When Linda came in, Joey was sitting in his chair, his sunglasses on, looking proud and happy. She fed him a milk shake.

After that, Joey would sit up in the chair for an hour each day. Then the nurses would gradually increase the sessions until he could sit up for as long as he desired. After a week, Joey surprised Danny with a phone call. Danny had not heard his brother speak for five months.

Joey, to everyone's surprise, had been able to talk immediately. His voice was lower, raspy, more careful than his normal voice, but it was clear, if just a touch uncertain. Danny told him to keep talking, then talked nonstop himself, hardly letting Joey get a word in edgewise. Joey beamed with delight.

Later that week he moved into a private room with a television. Posters and cards from well-wishers — pictures of planes and birds — lined his walls. Then the doctors decided to reduce his medication over two months, so Joey could eat. One evening Cherie, his favorite night nurse, ordered a pizza for them to share after his dressing change. The pizza would serve as a test of his ability to eat solids. He ate it ravenously, and kept it down. Linda considered this a milestone event. Cherie thought the pizza should have had more anchovies.

His back needed air to heal, so his nurses had to turn him on his stomach for two hours at a time, three times a day. Joey's body was almost fully covered with skin by this time — nearly seventy percent had been grafted — so his nurses concentrated on increasing his mobility and keeping the graft areas clean. Because infection could set in at any time, Joey had to bathe in a bleach solution. The forty-minute baths were very painful.

In her diary of this period, Linda writes that she is seated outside the operating room waiting for Joey. She is describing the operation and its complications, then in midstream begins writing about the kind of dog Joey would like. "It would have to be small and gentle and warm and devoted. I think it would have to be a Boston terrier. He loves them. I wonder where I'd get one. Must remember to talk to Mike about that." How had Linda arrived at the thought of a dog while writing about an operation? The diary entry is indicative of the optimistic mood she and Joey were in. Joey was talking and sitting up and even cracking jokes with the nurses. Linda was elated. She began to let her mind wander to the future.

Inside the operating room, there was concern about the next stage of grafting. Joey was in excessive pain and discomfort because they were replacing the skin on his back; this necessitated turning him on his stomach for hours at a time. The grafts were taking, but his body was running out of donor sites. The areas on his scalp and chest needed time to heal.

Cell biopsies — skin artificially cultured from Joey's cells — were not taking, and the doctors still had the better part of his lower legs and feet to cover. They concluded reluctantly that they might have to wait. The skin Joey had covered him enough to reduce the pain of contact with the air and to protect him from airborne bacterial infections.

The doctors also noted that Joey was having problems with his knee. The kneecap and surrounding cartilage and tendons had been destroyed in the fire. There was nothing there to fuse, and standard medical technology could not alleviate the problem. The doctors decided they could do nothing until Joey was covered with skin and even then they'd have to be careful. The knee could easily become infected if they tried to operate. He might still lose his leg.

After each operation, Joey could only sip fluids every two hours. He would lie on his stomach, waiting, in pain that neither morphine nor methadone could touch, his throat dry. He would beg Linda for something to quench his thirst, anything. She would wet a paper towel for him to suck on — but he couldn't swallow, or his stomach would try to throw up. After the operations, Linda would return to Halcyon House, go to her room, put a chair against the door — there were no locks — sit by the window and smoke a cigarette. (Smoking was taboo.) Alone in the room, Linda would wonder if Joey could go on much longer in Boston. He needed friends and family around to buoy his spirits. She and Joey hung in until September.

Then, at the beginning of September, the doctors went ahead with the operation to put a metal pin through Joey's knee in an attempt to fuse it. After the operation Joey had a new kind of physiotherapy. Ropes attached to a pulley lowered and raised the leg while Joey lay on his back. Splints attached to his legs held his feet upright. Without the splints, Joey's feet, which lacked tendons and muscles, would flop down so they stuck out like a ballerina's.

If his feet were to become locked in that position, Joey would not be able to walk again. They fuse there if they're not kept in a natural position with the splints. Linda would encourage Joey to endure the pain. "It doesn't make sense now, but trust me, it's worth it, Joey. You want to walk out of here, don't you?" Joey would nod his head and bear the pain.

If the most recent grafts were successful, most of Joey's body would be covered with skin by the end of September. There had been more than thirty skin-graft operations. Only the lower legs and feet, about eight percent Joey's body, remained open, sensitive and prone to infection.

Linda was optimistic, but Joey was not doing so well.

He was hallucinating again, and his leg became worse. He was alternately lucid and disoriented. Linda would rub his temples and try to distract him. She asked him to take deep breaths and go to a place that was free of pain. This technique had worked often in the past, but now he could only moan. Sometimes he wouldn't acknowledge the presence of Linda and the nurses. They worried that he was headed into a deep depression, which could in his case prove fatal. His will was the only thing that was keeping him alive.

Then Mike brought Danny to visit for a week. When he went back to Orillia, Danny would be sent to a foster home under care of the Children's Aid Society. He had been tossed around for the past five months, only this time he was being sent to stay with people he didn't know. Linda decided to go to Orillia with Danny, to meet the new foster parents. Still, the thought of the foster home cast a gloomy shadow over their week together.

One morning during Danny's visit, the pain in Joey's legs got worse. The doctors discovered that little mountains of calcium were growing in clusters along his lower legs. They were hard to the touch, and they pushed his body from the inside, stretching it, as they grew out. The doctors would discover later that the spurs were growing through the joints, splitting them apart. The inexplicable deposits grew and multiplied — each day a new group would appear. The doctors didn't know what to think — they had never witnessed a body in this shape before, so all they could do was test and identify the symptoms. They thought maybe the pin in Joey's knee had displaced some little chips of bone, which had somehow started calcifying. If the spurs could not be stopped, the legs might have to be amputated. They would have to wait and see. Joey remained in a hallucinatory world, moving in and out of consciousness.

He remembers those times, vividly. He remembers faces, ghoulish faces staring down at him lying in his bed. Sometimes they had bodies, sometimes just torsos. Then they would take on the form of someone he knew, a friend. He would be yelling down at the end of the bed, telling this phantom torturer to stop moving him, not to touch him there. These creatures of his confused imaginings would always reach out to do something to him.

He recalls that many times he would imagine Danny sitting and chatting when, all of a sudden, Danny would inadvertently move his leg or his arms. Joey would cry out to him, only to have a nurse rush over and persuade him that he was imagining, that it wasn't true. Once while he and Linda were talking, he turned and seemed to be struggling; he informed Linda that Danny was sitting on his legs, refusing to budge. It was deeply troubling to Linda to know that even when free of physically induced pain, his mind, altered by the massive amounts of chemicals, was inducing disturbing fantasies to parallel the physical torments he was daily undergoing in the outer world.

Mike would often sit with him, moving the pillow, telling him about the times they went fishing, reminding him of life on the western shores of Vancouver Island. Joey loved the west coast as much as Mike did, and Mike would tell him that someday they would return there together. You just got to be tough for a bit longer, he would say, and we'll get you there, buddy. He liked to call him buddy now. He wanted to call him son, but he had no right to that relationship.

Mike couldn't imagine how anyone could deal with such pain and refuse to give in. He wasn't that strong, and didn't know many who were. But here was this kid, struggling and surviving. Joey could have asked anything and Mike would gladly have done it. In an odd way it gave him strength, called him, as Father Michael might say, to love and to serve. But it didn't make it any easier.

Then there was Linda. She had invested her life energy into Joey. Nearly every ounce of it. What she had left she needed just to remain awake and coherent. Together they formed an ordinary little family that was dealing with an extraordinarily big event. There was a bond there, deep and unwavering, but the atmosphere was so oppressive. And who understood?

On September 11, Danny and Linda returned to Orillia so that Linda could meet Danny's new foster parents.

Marilyn, Danny's foster mother, was kind and understanding. Linda explained about Joey, and told Marilyn to call if she needed anything at all. She left, sadly, tears in her eyes, thinking that, with school stabilized, and a few friends dropping in on him, and the phone calls, they would all get through this. She returned to Boston early the next morning.

Joey's doctors sent him to Massachussets General, the teaching hospital across the street, so specialists could investigate his legs and try to sort out his severe digestive problems. Joey was again unable to keep anything down. His doctors had put his feeding tube deeper down, bypassing the digestive tract altogether. The doctors at Mass General thought the heavy doses of pain medication were destroying his stomach walls. They took him off his pain medicine but after two days he couldn't tolerate the pain. He was sick and frightened.

They resumed his medications, and Joey went back to

Shriners. A few days later, Mike and Linda met Anne and Camille, the parents of a young Boston-area boy whose body was burned extensively. Brian had been helping a friend clean off a trail bike. As always, they took the gas out of the tank and put it in a pail while cleaning the bike, a safety measure Brian had been taught by his father, Camille. Another young boy had come by and lit a match, which ignited the gas in the pail. When Brian tried to kick the burning pail away, it upturned and the gas flowed toward him. The flames engulfed his entire body.

Brian was burned as badly as Joey: third- and fourth-degree burns to ninety-five percent of his body, including his face. Anne and Camille were devastated. They arrived at Shriners in a state of panic and confusion — and longing. They wanted their son back. He had a young sister, who idolized him, and she wanted him back, too.

Linda wanted to say something to them, and when they talked there was an immediate bond. Mike and Camille became the best of friends, and so did Linda and Anne. Linda and Mike told Joey all about Brian, and Brian learned about Joey from his parents.

Brian struggled as Joey had. He was a survivor. His pain, like Joey's, was unbearable. He fought off infections, pneumonia, fluid imbalances. He went through an equal number of skin-grafting operations in a shorter period of time. For a while, like Joey, he couldn't talk. But he could blink once for yes and twice for no. More importantly, his parents could read his emotions through his eyes.

Shortly after Brian arrived, his nose, his lips and his ears dropped off. Only those who have been in such a situation can appreciate the bond that develops between a child and his parents. Nurses at Shriners are sensitive to it by virtue of having witnessed it many times over the years. Other people would think, "But surely, given his condition, it is better just to let him die.'' But they have not seen the love that is called forth in such situations. Anne and Camille did not give up.

One day Anne and Camille arrived on the ward and agreed to an operation that would close Brian's eyes. The doctors had to use the skin on his eyelids as a donor site. This done, they would cover his eyes with light gauze bandages. Anne and Camille continued talking to their son, but he could no longer communicate with them. They found inspiration in Joey. Like their son, he was a fighter, and he was winning the struggle. Joey had survived. Surely their son would survive as well.

On December 13, 1988, five months after he began the struggle, young Brian died.

Meanwhile, Joey was again having trouble breathing. One night his temperature fell to ninety-five degrees. Linda put a heated blanket over him, and his temperature rose to ninety-eight. Linda and Mike left the hospital, confident that he had managed to stabilize himself.

When they returned the next morning Joey was on a respirator again. He could no longer breathe unassisted. And he was being prepared for the operating room. The doctors had discovered that he had pneumonia again, and they were going to suction his lungs. His body was weak, his legs still covered with the painful calcium growths. Mike and Linda didn't return to Halcyon House for the next few days.

Linda thought Joey should get more medication. But Nancy, his pain nurse, was reluctant. The medications — morphine, methadone, Pavulon and other strong narcotics and sedatives — were destroying his organs. The doctors had never before had to give so much pain medicine to a young boy for so long.

Then, in the next week, Joey made another inexplicable recovery. Linda asked to take him outside. There was a risk of infection, and Joey was in pain, but the staff agreed that being outside would be psychologically beneficial.

So on September 27, almost two hundred days after the accident, Joey looked at the blue sky, felt a warm breeze caressing his face and the hot sun beaming down on him. Getting up, going outside, seeing with his own eyes the world his mother and Mike had been describing, helped to strengthen his will.

Mike took him outside again the next day. Some people had just left a meeting and were walking past. It had been ages since Joey saw the faces and heard the voices of happy, normal people. They were just walking and laughing and conversing with one another. His spirits rose.

That evening, Joey asked Mike whether he intended to stay with Linda forever. Mike reassured him, but Joey asked him to promise to take care of Linda. Mike promised.

In Orillia, the board of the Huronia Trust reminded Mike that the fund would pay for only two weeks in Boston; if he stayed longer, he would have to pay himself. Linda wanted Mike to stay, and they decided he would stay with Linda until Joey came home. They would find the money somewhere. There were still questions about the house that would be built, including location and contractual terms. Mike and Linda put the topic on hold.

Now Joey had to learn to live without pain medication, and he had to learn to walk. Dr. Briggs explained that Joey needed strength, and the only way to get that was to eat solid foods. But because of the strong painkillers, his stomach was still rejecting food. The doctors would have to take him off the medications.

They gradually reduced his medication; then, at the beginning of September, they ceased the medication altogether. Joey went into withdrawal. He begged and pleaded. He was unable to sleep, and he became irritable and depressed. The withdrawal lasted for three weeks. Then, slowly, Joey was able to keep solid foods down for longer periods of time. By October, the medical team was ready to begin walking him.

As part of his therapy, Joey would lie with his hands and legs raised. Each day they were raised higher, to maximize mobility and prevent constricture of the newly healing skin. His first faltering steps induced new pain. If anyone even mentioned walking, Joey's eyes glazed over with fear. For him, walking was a hollow victory.

Once Joey was able to be walked, Linda and Mike began to think of going home. Mike phoned the Hospital for Sick Children in Toronto to ask if they would be willing to take Joey. They would, they said, as soon as the doctors at Shriners were ready to send him. The Shriners medical team wanted to finish the skin grafts, which were almost complete. They thought Sick Kids could then continue his treatment, complete the remaining grafts on his lower leg, continue the second stage of therapy and plan with the family for Joey's future.

When Linda told Joey, he was overjoyed. Linda had not seen the light in his eyes so bright as at that moment. He was beside himself with happiness. For days afterward, nobody within hearing was unaware of Joey's impending departure. He joked with Cherie. He phoned everyone he knew in Canada. He told nurses, doctors and patients as they walked by.

On October 2, Joey again asked Linda for a mirror. He looked into it searchingly, first at his face, then at the rest of his body. He saw the marks on his face where the fire had tightened the skin and the scrubbing had left a light sheen. There were a few light scars. Where the grafts had taken on his arms and torso, the skin was gnarled and knotted. On his chest were inch-high mounds of flesh, which had not been destroyed by the fire. Everywhere else he saw ridges, indentations and scars. He saw where the flesh remained uncovered, and he saw the calcium deposits on his legs, and he wept.

"I look like a freak, Mom. I'll go home and people will look at me and laugh. I don't want people to laugh." Linda had been waiting to deal with this. She'd known that when his mind turned to home, it would turn to his body, and he would be afraid and repulsed.

"Joey," she said carefully, rehearsing in her mind the effects of her words before she spoke them, "your face is fine. The mirror distorts certain things. I want you to look at my face in the mirror and then look directly at me." He did, and there was indeed a difference. "You do have marks, some scars, but your face is beautiful, Joey, and your eyes are clear and the only time people will laugh is when you laugh, Joey, because when you laugh your eyes light up and your joy is infectious. No one will laugh at your face. But Joey, you are right about your body. It's in bad shape. And many people will stare at you, and make cruel and insensitive comments. They may even laugh. Neither you nor I can stop that. But we can work on it together. We'll find the best available technology and the best equipment and the latest research and we'll do the best we can with what we've got. The important thing is you, Joey, and we are still together as a family and we love each other deeply. The rest we will deal with together."

It was both a good sign and a sad one. In the second stage of recovery from a burn, a victim begins to think about his body, about the rejection he will face from his peers. Joey's wish to see his body was a sign that the long death watch was over.

As much as Mike and Linda wanted to leave, saying good-bye was not easy. They had come to know so many people. They were especially fond of Anne, the receptionist, whose cheer and compassion had helped them through many difficult periods. They had come to know the cleaning staff, the kitchen personnel, security guards and orderlies. In her joy, Linda told them all repeatedly that Joey was leaving, then remembered that she had to say goodbye and how much she would miss them. The friends they had made at Halcyon House had a going-away gathering. They were surprised at the number of friends they had made in Boston.

The hardest parting was from Father Michael. He had participated in the vigil and made it bearable for all of them. Father Michael gave Mike and Linda a farewell dinner.

Tears flowed easily during those last weeks. But with the tears there was great joy. Joey remained alert and excited. He endured the pain, even walked, with moderate assistance, for ten steps, to his and everyone's immense satisfaction and disbelief. He would sit for hours, which weeks earlier he had not been able to do. His depression, irritability and sleeplessness vanished.

Linda packed up all the gifts, posters and mementos they had gathered during their stay. There were letters from Australia and New Zealand, from Buckingham Palace and Canada's prime minister, Brian Mulroney, from Nia, from mothers and grandmothers and children. The books about aviation and the flying paraphernalia were special to Joey. He loved men in uniform and the planes they maneuvered far above the earth.

His most prized possession was the Canadian Snowbird uniform and wings, given to him by Commander Dennis Beselt, the 1988 Canadian Snowbird Captain. He also had some military mementos from his cadet squadron in Orillia and from Canadian Armed Forces officials from Cold Lake, Alberta. These were carefully packed in special boxes.

Joey remembers clearly when Commander Dennis Beselt had come down in the summer. The thought of it had lifted his spirits. To Joey, the Snowbirds and the Canadian Air Force pilots are almost mythic personages. Before they were to arrive, he had Linda cover him neatly, and asked if he could refrain from his therapy so he would be sure to be relatively free of pain. He asked if the sheets covering him could be ironed. He felt in some way that he was on inspection and wanted thing just right. He was honored. He kept his cap by his bed-side and waited.

Days before they were to have arrived, Linda received a phone call informing her that they had to reschedule the awards ceremony due to the death of two members of the Snowbirds.

She was reluctant to tell Joey. He had lived in anticipation of the moment ever since the news first came. Their death might overwhelm him. She toyed with the idea of telling him something else had delayed them, but in the end she told him the truth. He did cry, but not for himself. "I didn't know what to say. It was so sad. I wanted to tell them I was sorry, but I could only lie in my bed at that time and there was nothing I could do."

Two weeks later, Beselt arrived and presented Joey with the uniform and welcomed him to their fraternity. He was now one of that honored and rare breed of aviator, Beselt informed him, a Canadian Snowbird. It was a moving ceremony. Joey asked about the height and speed at which they flew and what formations they enjoyed and what the interior of their plane looked like. He wanted to know whether he would be able to fly with them. And Beselt answered that he would fly just as soon as he got out and was well. They would welcome him aboard as they would a brother. They talked of the fabulous exploits of pilots the world over, and then Beselt left the young boy to dream of that which he desired most.

Linda recalled all this with Joey as they set about packing things for the trip home. Joey wanted to wear the Snowbird uniform on the trip home, but they couldn't get it over the bandages without cutting it — which was unthinkable.

After much deliberation, Joey decided to wear the Bruins T-shirt the Toronto *Sun* had sent him, as well as the hat he had received from Brett, a young friend at Shriners. He also wore his sunglasses.

As the stretcher was wheeled into the waiting area, nurses

and hospital staff were everywhere. They had prepared a large cake, and everyone gathered around to congratulate the family and wish Joey well. Joey asked to use the intercom to say goodbye. He was happy, and holding back tears. They wheeled him close to the intercom.

"Hello, everyone, this is Joe," he said, as if anyone could mistake his voice. "I just want to say goodbye and thank all of you for taking care of me. I hope everyone else gets better, too, and goes home soon. I will miss you and always remember you. Thank you and goodbye."

Monica, Sue, Jack and Cherie, Anne the receptionist, Bill the security guard, Doctors Briggs and Remensyder, the residents and numerous Shriners took turns saying goodbye, some brushing away tears. One nurse spoke for many when she told Linda she had not believed Joey would leave Shriners alive.

The journey leading to this departure had been remarkable. Joey was the most badly burned child the doctors at the institute had ever treated. He was a symbol of the advancements made in the past ten years in treating burn patients. A decade ago he would have died. Five years ago, he would have stood a limited chance. Today he was alive due to the reconstructive techniques pioneered at centers such as Shriners.

At 11:30 AM on October 24, 1988, seven months and two weeks after he had arrived, Joey Philion was flying over the rooftops of Boston, sunglasses firmly in place, hat on, smiling from ear to ear as the plane leveled off at 22,000 feet and set its course for Canada, for home.

CHAPTER SIX

Linda had been only incidentally aware of the public's response to her son's struggle. She expected to meet Danny, Mike and a few relatives at the airport, drive with them to the hospital and settle into a new routine as quickly as possible. She was in for a surprise.

Tens of thousands of people across the nation had followed the story of Joey's epic struggle. The tale had first been told in the Orillia *Packet and Times* by Jeff Day, then gradually spread south to the more populous areas of southern Ontario, across the border, then to Boston and New York. By the end of the first year, Joey had made headlines in England, Australia, Singapore and Tokyo. He had become a significant media event.

Through the newspapers and television, people had sat with Linda at Joey's bedside. They were almost as excited as she was about Joey's return. They wanted to tell him he had moved and inspired them in countless ways. Responding to the demand, reporters turned out in droves to see Joey.

On the day of Joey's return, numerous radio and television stations approached Mike, wanting to film Mike and Danny as they greeted Joey. It was a day of celebration, and they wanted to record it properly, they told Mike. But Mike wanted them to stand back. This was a private affair.

As the air ambulance approached the Toronto Island Airport runway, nearly a hundred reporters waited at the fence. There were people from just about every major paper in the country. Mike and Danny were jostled to the outer edge of the crowd.

Trailing the paramedics and nurses who were accompanying Joey, Linda stepped out of the plane and into a tangle of microphones, wires, cameras and persistent reporters. "How is he?" "What's it like to be home?" "What will you do first?" She wanted to say he was very sick, that it had been a long and harrowing flight, that they had to get to the hospital. But the words stuck in her throat.

Reporters tried to surround Joey, to get close enough to capture the first words of the returning hero. Microphones were shoved at his face. Flash bulbs went off. Joey's pained smile as he was wheeled across the tarmac to the waiting ambulance would touch the hearts of the nation as people watched the six o'clock news.

Linda could see Mike and Danny in the distance. Mike found it impossible to get through, but Danny made a beeline between the knees of the reporters, straight to Joey and his mother. He stood before his brother beaming, as reporters strained to capture their conversation. Microphones were pressed in toward them. "Hey, get back from my mom and my brother," yelled Danny as he realized they were being pressed in. Linda was pleased to be home and to be seeing Danny. She wanted to savor the moment, just as she wanted to reach out and embrace Mike, who had by now reached her side, but that would have to wait. She made a brief statement about how happy they were to be back in Canada among family and friends, then headed for the waiting ambulance.

Danny had been given a microphone and tape recorder by Trish Wood, an enterprising CBC radio journalist who had primed him on the art of interviewing. In the ambulance, Danny and Joey talked nonsense. Danny, with a microphone in his hand, asked silly questions of Joey and got equally silly answers. They were thus engaged, with Mike and Linda sitting off to the side, as the reporters, cameras in hand, pressed their faces against the window trying desperately to get that last picture or word from the family. Danny gloatingly waved the microphone and held up the recorder. He and Joey laughed as the ambulance pulled away. (The CBC did not air their interview.)

The reporters followed the ambulance to the hospital, exhibiting once again the pack mentality that frightened as much as it surprised and impressed Linda. Joey couldn't understand what all the fuss was about. As he put it, "I thought that it was really nice that so many people would come to see us, but I don't know why they are all like that. I think it would be better maybe if they come in one at a time."

In Boston, Linda and Joey had been alone but for an occasional reporter from the CBC, the *Packet and Times* in Orillia or CKVR television, Barrie. Linda remembered when Jeff Day came to Boston. He had seen Joey's pain and had interviewed him sensitively. Linda thought, naively, that all reporters were like Jeff, or like Linda Hurst, from the *Toronto Star*, or like Michelle Rao, from CKVR.

But when the family entered the emergency room at Sick Kids hospital, Linda encountered another large group of frenzied reporters. They crowded the hallways to get a look at Joey. The family wanted only to deal with Joey and the medical staff. They wanted, as did the nurses and doctors, to make sure he was okay after the long trip. In the hectic atmosphere, in new and unfamiliar surroundings, Joey and the family needed all the time they could get to understand what was happening, to make the transition from Boston to Toronto.

But as she walked through the corridors holding Mike's arm, Linda realized that her private nightmare had become a public spectacle. Joey had become a celebrity.

Dr. Clark, the plastic surgeon who had convinced Linda to transfer Joey to Boston, welcomed Joey to Sick Kids. He was amazed, as he looked at the tired, gaunt face of the boy who was lying on the bed, that Joey had actually survived. The odds against it, when Joey left, were astounding, but here he was, weak still, but definitely alive. Dr. Clark wondered how Joey had had the will to withstand the lifesaving medical assaults he underwent in Boston. He wondered, too, how much they would be able to do for him at Sick Kids. How much further would they be able to take him? He and his medical team looked closely at Joey's prognosis in the next weeks. First he needed rest and a healthy diet to build up his skeletal frame.

A nurse and a physiotherapist had flown to Toronto with Joey. They described the therapy Joey had received at Shriners, and showed videos to illustrate their methods. One video showed two nurses, one on each side of Joey, raising and lowering his legs for thirty minutes. Joey was screaming in agony the whole time. They explained their rationale for their aggressive therapies: if left to themselves, severely burned patients tended to close in on themselves, in order to avoid the pain caused by movement of any kind. But the pain would ease as the joints loosened and the skin became more elastic. The doctors and nurses at Shriners had found that the will of the patient was often mobilized along with the body.

The nurse and physiotherapist were worried that they had not made a good impression. They thought the team at Sick Kids believed Shriners' therapies to be too radical.

That wasn't unusual, the nurse later told Linda. Often different hospitals use different techniques. The aggressive therapeutic techniques Shriners is noted for are not standard at many other hospitals.

Betty Courmier, head nurse at Toronto's Hospital for Sick Children's Burn Unit, came in to talk to Mike and Linda. She had been at Sick Kids when the new burn unit was built; and after almost half a century of nursing, she knew nearly everything there was to know about burn patients. She also knew all about Joey: she had followed his progress at Shriners. Linda and Mike were impressed.

In her kind, firm way — someone once described her as a cross between Florence Nightingale and an army sergeant — Betty explained the procedures on her ward.

She wanted to let Joey relax, recover from the excitement of the trip. They would all have to get used to new routines, which would probably unnerve them, but she and her nurses would help them all make the transition. Then she explained that there would only be two scheduled visitors allowed each week. Linda and Mike stared at one another in disbelief. Two visits a week? They had been spending almost ten hours a day with Joey, sometimes more. Joey would go crazy if he spent so much time alone. A press conference had been scheduled for that evening, and Linda and Mike didn't want to argue with the hospital staff just before it. They would discuss visiting privileges after the meeting.

That evening, Linda told reporters that Joey was fine after the trip and that they were both extremely happy to be home. She thanked everyone, and said there was still a long way to go. Someone asked about the trust fund, and the possibility of a new house being built in Orillia. Linda declined to comment. Then came the question she would hear again and again in the next few months: "Do you think your son is a hero?" Linda hesitated before replying, then said that she didn't understand why Joey's story had touched so many people, but it would be better to ask those who were touched. She was just happy her son was alive.

After the press conference, Linda and Mike got lost in the large hospital. They wandered down a maze of corridors filled with white-coated lab technicians, orderlies and doctors. Sick Kids didn't have the intimacy of the thirty-bed Shriners Institute. The burn unit at Sick Kids was a long corridor with rooms on either side. Pictures of smiling bunnies and bears in pastel colors graced the walls. The suffering here went on behind closed doors. They had to gown up to enter Joey's room to prevent the spread of MRSA, a low-level infection that lies dormant in patients who have been weak and hospitalized for months, but which can be spread to other sick patients. It was so different from Shriners, which had been open; there, parents and nurses shared the ward equally with the children. Betty was right. It would take time to get used to the changes.

Joey was sleeping when they entered his room. Without the sunglasses and the hat he looked frail and sick. Linda began to cry as she looked at his face. So much suffering in such a small body. She kissed him lightly on the cheek and was rewarded with a flicker of a smile.

Then they left.

The next morning, October 25, Hans Gerhardt, general manager of Toronto's luxurious Sutton Place Hotel, phoned to offer Mike and Linda free lodging for three months. They had known that finding a place was going to be a problem, but they hadn't found time to work out the details. Friends and relatives had offered accommodation, but none of the places was large enough to accommodate both of them. And Linda and Mike felt comfortable only with each other. Mike had applied at a temporary work group, and he thought that within a month he could save enough money to rent a small apartment. Meanwhile, Hans Gerhardt's call was welcome news. He suggested they move in as soon as possible.

Hans Gerhardt is an amiable man, with a slight German accent. He came from a working-class family that immigrated to Canada to find a better life, and he doesn't forget his past easily. He remembers what it was like "to be down on your luck, looking for that cubic centimeter of chance that was going to change it." He found it. As a result he remains active in community organizations and fund-raising events for good causes.

When he read about the Hawkinses and their long struggle, he thought the hotel, which was close to the hospital, would be ideal.

Sutton Place, his domain, is one of the most exclusive hotels in Toronto. Marble floors. Murals and classical paintings gracing the walls. Rich, brocaded tapestries and rugs of the finest weave everywhere. Mercedes, Jaguars and Rolls-Royces lining the driveway. The doormen wear fur coats in the winter, and speak with an array of accents that show the international flavor of the place. Linda and Mike had rarely seen anything like it. And at a whopping $240 per night for the economy rooms, they hadn't thought they ever would. They would have settled for a basement closet in such a setting. They felt uncomfortable riding in the elevator surrounded by well-appointed ladies with furs and diamonds, and men in three-piece suits. But the room was magnificent and private, and they would be close to Joey. Hans made it clear that it was a gift freely given, that they in turn would one day repay someone else, just as he had done in his time.

During the next few weeks calls and invitations came in from people across Canada. Friends they hadn't seen for years called; family and relatives vied for their time. Strangers called to give advice and to congratulate Joey on his recovery. Strangers offered flowers and small gifts for Joey.

Public service organizations across Canada asked to present awards and tributes to Joey. Boy Scouts, Air Cadets, Kiwanis and Kinsmen clubs, volunteer associations, police and military associations, provincial governments, the federal government — every conceivable group based on the ideals of service and self-sacrifice, valor and bravery. They all thought Joey embodied their ideals. Joey was both honored and confused by the constant stream of people who came to award, congratulate, honor or simply welcome him back. He had acted over the last seven months with unselfconscious determination and courage. His reward was to live again with his mother and family.

Through delicate negotiation, Linda and Mike had persuaded Betty Courmier to allow daily visits from family, friends and well-wishers. Linda and Mike were able to come and go at will. It was a workable compromise.

Three weeks after their return to Toronto, Linda received a call from Delsie McCan of Orillia: her husband, Ken, had decided to build a house for the family. The project was being organized by Ken, and hundreds of people in Orillia had offered services and material so the house could be built.

Linda was speechless. She remembers hanging up the phone and turning to Mike. "They're going to build us a house, Mike. They're building it for Joey. They're not going to take any money from anyone, not the trust fund, not us, not anyone." She wondered if Mike shouldn't phone back just to confirm what she had heard.

The next day Linda's lawyer, Doug Sparks, came to talk to them about the house. He said Mike and Linda had to meet with the architect and other people involved in the project. There were also some legal details to be decided before work could begin. He said the architect would talk to the hospital medical experts so the house could be fitted properly for Joey. As well, he explained that the house would be in Joey's name, so none of Linda's and Mike's debtors could place a lien against it. Linda's father would have to relinquish his mortgage.

Linda knew that her parents had been feeling left out and unwanted since the fire. Linda had neglected family and friends in her response to Joey. Even Mike, whom she needed and loved, felt that neglect; he knew her energy was invested primarily in Joey. Linda's parents had been hurt by her apparent abandonment of them. When Linda explained all this, Delsie McCan phoned Linda's father. He agreed to relinquish the mortgage and legal claim to the title, and the house was placed in Joey's name.

Linda and Mike were uncertain whether Joey or the family could live on Cleveland Avenue again. Would it not be filled with unwanted memories? But home was the next major hurdle, and Joey had a home to go to. Without it they had nothing, and it was possible that Joey could end up in an institution. The people of Orillia, on their own initiative, would build Joey a house — a dream house from the look of the architect's plans — which tended to confirm the belief that Joey would soon be going home. Together they had survived this ordeal and, with much support, they were going to become a family once again.

Within a week, Linda and Mike were at the site watching the crew lay the foundation.

Memories came flooding back. Linda saw again the burning house, heard the roar of the fire, saw Joey smoldering, pleading, and herself running toward him, screaming. She recalled this as she spoke uncomfortably with the men around her, who were busy pouring blocks of cement and piling lumber. They were doing it for free, out of the goodness of their hearts in response to Joey's inspiration and need. Whether she wanted to live on Cleveland Avenue or not, she was here now and Joey would be here soon.

Ken McCan told her how the project had started from a small ad placed in the paper. He and Delsie had been sitting down to lunch one day thinking about the plight of the

Hawkinses and wondering what they could do to relieve it. They had heard, as just about everybody had, about the trust fund's reluctance to finance the building of a house, and they knew it had something to do with medical and legal entanglements. But Ken and Delsie, like many Orillians, wanted to do something for Joey. But what? It was only as they sat together at lunch one day that a comment from Delsie sparked the idea in Ken's mind: "Of course, we can build the house."

Ken, an electrician, thought, if I'm willing to do the electrical work for free, and I know others who would contribute, how many more would offer their services? He wrote a small piece for the papers outlining his views; within minutes of the notice appearing, the telephone started ringing, and it didn't stop for months.

What Linda was witnessing, he told her, was the result of a feeling that had been building in the community.

Linda thought of Linda Young next door. If she and Linda had had a complex relationship before the fire, it had intensified after. It was Linda, after all, who had saved her son's life, and taken Danny into her home after the fire. They had been getting along well during their last few meetings — as infrequent as those meetings were — and she wanted to talk with her. They spoke of the house and the fire and Joey's progress. For Linda Young, it wasn't easy to live with the memory of Joey's smoldering body, his skin coming off in her hands. Who could possibly understand the weight of her own memories? She and Linda and Joey were bound together by that day in March.

Linda felt she could talk to her neighbor about one thing that had been bothering her since she had become aware of the attention Joey was receiving from the press and public. Linda had noticed that some people were sensitive, inspired. But one letter she had received insinuated that the Hawkins family was in some way exploiting Joey's tragedy, that they were somehow benefiting from it. Linda Young said some people did believe Mike and Linda were somehow taking advantage. People expected Linda and Mike to be perfect, she explained. There would always be people who spread rumors about someone's past or present. She counseled Linda not to worry about the rumor mongers—just to care for Joey; the rest would take care of itself.

Meanwhile, Joey was lying in isolation on the eighth floor of the Hospital for Sick Children. The medical team had isolated him because he carried MRSA.

Joey knew no one. He didn't like the isolation. He didn't know his doctors or nurses yet.

The medical team explained to Joey and to Linda and Mike that adjustments, even small ones, are difficult for rehabilitating burn patients. Joey had to make a major adjustment. People who have grown familiar with the procedures of one hospital, with the rhythm of its routines, are disturbed by changes. In time, everyone would adjust.

At first, Linda and Mike had difficulty accepting this rationale; they had come to believe in Shriners' aggressive style of physiotherapy, and Joey was getting little of that as far as they could tell. But within two or three weeks, Joey seemed to have adjusted. Dr. Clark and Dr. Zuker, the chief surgeon, had decided Joey needed a rest from the grueling daily routines he had performed in Boston. The nurses went easy while they assessed his status and determined his prognosis. No physiotherapy, no extensive movements, no chair to sit in, no operations.

Joey was happy to be free of the daily round of pain, and happier still to be seeing friends and relatives. The psychological benefits were undeniable, even remarkable. Linda and Mike began to relax.

When Linda told Joey about the house, he again asked why all these people were being so kind. He was thinking of the house and the gifts and tributes that continued to pour in from across the world, as well as the press that came to see him or called on a daily basis. Linda explained that the house was being built so that he could go home.

"And what is it you want more than anything else in the world, Joey?" Linda would ask.

And Joey would tell her with a glow in his eye, "I just want to go home."

Joey had no fears or misgivings about living above the ruins of the fire. He was able to speak freely about the fire, without obvious fear or regret. Linda could not come to terms with his stoic acceptance. But he had, or so it seemed to Linda, accepted the fire and the consequences.

Ironically, as she began to share with others the burden of caring, and as Joey began to feel strong and positive, Linda began to weaken, emotionally and physically. She had constant headaches, and she began to feel as if something were draining the energy from her body. Sometimes she couldn't sleep; at other times, she would fall asleep wherever she happened to be. In Boston, despite her rigorous schedule, she had never been sick.

Joey sensed the change in her. "Mom," he would say, "you should go and rest. It's too much for you to stay in hospital. You're weak. I'll be okay."

She went to see Dan McCan, a burn unit social worker who had been assigned to Joey's case. McCan had years of experience in dealing with burn victims. He was aware of the stresses parents undergo during a patient's recovery. When Linda told him how she was feeling, he listened carefully. Then he said her response might be normal. He suggested that she try some relaxation techniques. In the next few weeks, McCan listened to Linda and helped her to relax deeply. The symptoms of fatigue and anxiety became manageable, then gradually subsided. Linda enjoyed the trancelike states the relaxation sessions induced, because she could experience the peace that had eluded her since the day of the fire. She wondered if Joey could be taught to relax, and she asked McCan about it. He said he would certainly like to try once he got to know Joey better. He explained that children and adolescents were usually good candidates because they're less fearful about giving control to someone else and are closer to the twilight world of the unconscious into which one descends in the relaxed state. It was possible that Joey could learn to control his pain through relaxation, and McCan certainly wanted to give it a try.

Mike was less eager to attempt these relaxation techniques than Linda. It just wasn't the kind of activity he engaged in, but he wanted to find some method of coping. Joey had touched the heart of almost everyone who heard about him. He had certainly touched and changed Mike's life, and it didn't look like things were going to get any less complex in the foreseeable future.

During December, as media coverage increased, more and more people began appearing at the hospital. They would phone from downstairs when Linda was visiting Joey on the eighth floor and ask if they could visit with him or meet the family.

The hospital would try to screen the calls, but the well-wishers were ingenious. Joey appeared to have been the grandson and nephew and brother and cousin of hundreds of people. (Joey's real relatives sometimes had trouble convincing nurses that they were indeed who they said they were.)

Some of these visitors went to great lengths to see Joey. One gentle older woman visited the hospital frequently, in an attempt to get to see Joey or his parents. On one visit the kindly

but insistent woman was informed that Joey's mother was
sitting in the waiting room. The older woman went right over,
and during their conversation she invited Linda to dinner.

A few days later, while Linda was visiting Joey, she was told
that she had a visitor downstairs.

As she approached the lobby, Linda saw the older woman,
looking radiant with happiness, standing next to a rabbi. They
were beside a table laid with white linen, the finest china, in-
laid silverware. The woman and the rabbi had set up an entire
seven-course traditional Jewish dinner in the lobby of the
hospital. Linda was astonished and pleased. She immediately
went to get Mike.

A few minutes later, Linda and Mike sat side by side at the
sumptuous table. The dinner was delicious.

In early December Linda began to wonder when Joey would
be fully covered with new skin. There had been only a small
area of his legs left to cover when he arrived in Toronto. Boston
had done a lot in a short time, and Linda had anticipated,
wrongly, that the Hospital for Sick Children would work at
the same pace. She knew that when Joey had skin everywhere
she could take him outside. He would get a psychological boost
from going out, and he would heal more quickly physically
— the cure for MRSA is fresh air. Then the doctors could per-
form the delicate surgery needed to give him more flexibility
in areas where the skin had contracted from the scarring. After
that, the medical team could assess the state of Joey's legs.

Linda wanted to know everything about his legs, especially
his knee, which was still causing him a lot of pain. Could the
doctors fuse it? Could anything be done? Did the doctors in
Toronto think he wouldn't walk? Is that why they were not
getting him up? Dr. Zuker, when she could find him, would
refer her to the orthopedic surgeon. The orthopedic surgeon
kept postponing their meeting.

Linda was also worried because the splints on Joey's hands

and feet were frequently removed. The Boston therapists had told her the splints would keep the feet upright, stop them from pulling down and flopping out. Linda asked the nurses about the splints; the nurses assured her that everything was fine. They didn't approve of the splints made in Boston, and were awaiting the delivery of new ones.

In seven months in Boston, Joey had forty-one operations. In Toronto, in two months, he had only two. Betty Courmier, the head nurse, tried to reassure Linda. But she couldn't give detailed answers to the specific questions Linda was asking. Linda looked at Joey. His face had lost its lean, gaunt look; he was gaining weight. He seemed to be happier. All undeniable signs of progress. But Linda's questions remained unanswered.

CHAPTER SEVEN

A deep bond had developed between Joey and Nia, the young girl who had written to him from a town near Barrie. At first, to Joey, Nia was a literary creation, a fantasy. But if Nia was a fantasy to Joey, what was Joey to Nia?

Nia knew him only through the media, but she thought she had a clear idea of who he had become since the fire. Nia believed he was valiant. She thought his spirit would rise above the frailty of his body.

One day Linda asked Joey if he would like to meet Nia. She had gotten Nia's phone number from reporter Jim Wilkes.

Nia answered the telephone. She said she would like to see Joey; she would ask her father to drive her down.

Nia arrived with her parents, Peter and Bran, and Mike met them in the lobby. Then Mike took Nia upstairs. Both Joey and Nia were nervous. Mike decided to leave them alone; he returned to the waiting room, and talked to Peter and Bran.

When Linda arrived thirty minutes later, she told Bran how

much Joey had enjoyed Nia's letters. In a very few visits, their friendship grew. For Nia, the visiting hours went by too quickly, and Joey agreed.

As winter set in, Joey began to think about going out to be with his family on Christmas Day. For weeks he suffered through his therapy buoyed by that one blissful thought. If the nurses wanted him to do five leg lifts he would do ten. If they wanted him to hold his arms out for fifteen minutes, he would go twenty. If he was strong, and if the doctors saw progress, they would let him go to the hotel with Linda and Mike and Danny.

Linda had seen his spirits fade in the aftermath of an unkept promise or an anticipated positive event in his life. She longed for it as much as he did, but she left it an open-ended possibility, just as the doctors had. As the date drew closer, she could see the doctors becoming increasingly more positive about his being ready to go out. By the second week of December, she felt certain that he would be allowed to venture out and began stating it with conviction among family and close friends. Christmas was a prelude to going home, one more step along the road to whatever destiny awaited them outside the confines of the hospital.

Hans Gerhardt once again stepped in to help the family. Joey could be moved in a modified stretcher, which was too big for the Hawkinses' room. Gerhardt offered the use of a ballroom large enough to accommodate a feast. He would also arrange the feast himself. And if Joey was not well enough to go to the hotel, Gerhardt would arrange that a traditional Christmas feast be sent to Joey and his family at the hospital.

A week before Christmas, Linda and Mike were told that Joey was strong enough to go out for Christmas.

Mike phoned Danny and Hans Gerhardt. Linda told Joey. They decided to invite John Parfect, a man Joey had met in Boston. Joey hadn't heard from John in weeks, and was worried about him.

John, like Joey, had survived a terrible fire during his adolescence. That had been more than thirty-five years ago. John told CBC journalist Trish Wood that he felt a bond with Joey, a bond he couldn't explain. John met Joey when Joey was becoming concerned about his body, asking Linda for mirrors and worrying about looking like a freak.

John and Joey talked for a long time about pain, John encouraging Joey to put up with it, reassuring him that it would gradually diminish, then one day disappear.

Then, knowing that Joey wanted to see his body but was too polite to ask, John offered to show him the effects of the fire. Even thirty-five years after the fire, John's skin was scarred, discolored and contracted.

It was precisely what Joey needed to see. John was a survivor. He was more fit than the average person — he jogged four miles a day — and he was successful. In John Joey saw living proof that there was life after the fire. Unfortunately, John couldn't make it to the Christmas party.

On Christmas day, at two forty-five, the ambulance arrived. Joey could barely contain himself; he was radiant. He was in a special stretcher chair designed to keep him comfortable and flexible during the holiday.

The media turned out in full force, and they were unusually sensitive. Linda asked them not to take photographs or interfere with the family; everyone complied.

Hans Gerhardt's chefs had prepared a traditional Christmas feast with turkey and stuffing, cranberry sauce, roast potatoes, turnips, carrots, plum pudding and a wide assortment of fruits.

The staff at the hotel raised banners of welcome and colored streamers and piled the presents from across the country high under a tall green pine. The family, the nurses, the paramedics and a few friends dined and laughed and presented gifts to each other and made speeches and toasted each other with champagne.

They call it the house that love built, and they are proud of it. When Joey needed a house, they built it. They say it was that simple. But it wasn't.

Men, women and children, the townspeople of Orillia, wanted to help the Hawkins family. Although the family had not been in Orillia long, the children had gone to local schools; Mike and Linda had shopped at the local stores and worked in town. Within days of the fire, the people of Orillia had begun to help the Hawkins family.

The original trust fund, established by people in town, had become too complex for its own board members to control, despite repeated attempts to help the family. The board members did most of the work on their own time, for free. But the money the fund collected was becoming bogged down in legal niceties. In the end, the people of Orillia decided to circumvent the fund's bureaucratic difficulties. They began to build a house for Joey Philion. The project was masterminded by Ken McCan, who worked untold hours, organizing workers, coordinating the materials builders and suppliers were giving freely. And he was adamant about not accepting money. Some people sent money anyway, and he and his wife Delsie sent it back. The response to the project was overwhelming. Boxes of supplies arrived unannounced just when they were needed.

Workers and architects labored over the details that went into the house, which was built with Joey constantly in mind. A central system connects the house to the fire department, police station and hospital. There is an elevator to help Joey move from the first floor to the second. The bath, actually a Jacuzzi, is enormous, so it can accommodate Joey's special bathing chair. The masonry, the oak throughout the kitchen, the incidental supplies in the house are of high quality. The house is both a home and a rehabilitation center. It would have cost nearly half a million dollars to build. But it was built for free, and it was finished within three cold winter months. Joey's home was ready.

After Christmas Joey talked of nothing but going out.

They were waiting for a specially designed wheelchair for Joey. While they waited, Linda encouraged him to move his arms back and forth and to lift his legs even higher than his physiotherapists asked him to. When the chair arrived, he would be strong enough to go outside. If he didn't move, he would stiffen up. But Joey began to have long periods of depression. He lacked the motivation to continue therapy.

Joey's knee was a constant source of pain. The doctors were still uncertain whether there was enough bone or tendon for them to fuse. The physiotherapists made Joey walk. They walked him into the tub room for his daily bath, but the pain was great. They didn't know if he would be able to walk on his own again. His screams of agony could be heard down the halls. Walking had once been a goal of the therapy. Now they concentrated on increasing his mobility. In Boston the therapists had worked with Joey for two hours each day, and Joey had been progressing rapidly. The medical team in Toronto didn't want to cause him pain; they thought he had suffered enough. But Linda thought that with less aggressive therapy, Joey's rate of progress was gradually diminishing. She and Mike talked to Dan McCan, the social worker, who assured Linda that everything being done for Joey was in his best interest. He encouraged her to look ahead to when Joey could go home.

Joey had been isolated in his room for more than three months. The daily round of friends and relatives had cheered him, as did the many special awards and tributes he received from groups as diverse as the Toronto Maple Leafs, law enforcement agencies, the Governor General's office and numerous smaller organizations. He was especially honored when military organizations paid him tribute. Whenever someone in uniform, such as his squadron leaders, came to present him with an award, he felt both humbled and proud. For days afterward he would mention it to anyone who came in and show them the certificate that he had Linda hang on his wall. But he was desperate to go outside. He wanted to see other kids. He wanted anything that was beyond his four walls. But there was no chair and therefore no way out. He was stuck there. "I'll never get out of here, Mom," he would complain, and sink deeper into himself.

As always, with Linda sitting on the side of the bed, and with Joey's head turned toward her, Linda would help him sip on his juice or cold drink. He couldn't do it himself with his arms locked at the elbow. She would speak into his ear. She would tell him to hang on and that soon they'd be able to take him out.

The media were still calling and reporting on Joey's progress. Each day they would ask how he was, what he was thinking, and each day Linda would tell them he was making slow progress and would soon be going home; the family hoped and looked forward to that day. It was always the same questions, to which Linda responded as well as she was able. But what could she say other than that he was doing fine? There were no operations scheduled. The two operations done in Toronto had not been entirely successful. Joey's lower legs remained uncovered by skin, and were healing slowly on their own. Joey was in a holding pattern.

In mid-January, Danny went to stay with Debby and Roy, two old friends of Linda's and Mike's. The move worked out for everyone. Since early childhood, Danny had occasionally had mild epileptic seizures. The seizures were a cause of concern. (In November and December he had been troubled because the family was close, yet he couldn't stay with them. He spent every weekend in Toronto with Linda and Mike; it was difficult to tear him away from Joey's bedside.)

A few people were unhappy about the house in Orillia. Why was it so large? Why hadn't the Hawkins family been more directly involved? The trust fund continued to grow, under the direction of Roy McMurtry's law office.

Then some of the discontent was reported by the press. The feelings that had surfaced shortly after Joey's return from Boston began to dominate. How much were Linda and Mike getting, some people asked. And were they exploiting a tragic situation? Had Joey really saved his brother or tried to save his mother? How had the fire actually started? Some people even suggested that Linda and Mike had made up the story. Wasn't Linda the source of the media's — and therefore the public's — information? Wasn't she the one who said he had tried to save her?

The mistrust and uncertainty began to spread. Builders at the house began to murmur about the ingratitude of the Hawkins family; they consoled themselves by saying the house was really for Joey.

Linda was disturbed when people presumed to call her son a liar. She was tired. The pressure and stress of the past year were accumulating. She had thought it would get easier with time; instead it was getting worse.

Mike and Linda had nothing to say to people who questioned what Joey had done. There was no question, for them. They were the ones who had lived through it. And they would have traded it in a moment for their life before the fire.

On February 18, Joe received a visit from his old friend Cherie, who had been his nurse in Boston. She was in Toronto for her holidays. She walked into Joey's room at Sick Kids and said, "I'm here to raise your arms, Joey." They both laughed. They talked for a while, then Joey fell asleep.

After Cherie left, Linda talked to Betty Courmier again. She expressed her worries about Joey's therapy, then said she wanted to take him out for walks. They had been promised a chair five months ago. Where was it? Why wasn't Sick Kids doing anything for Joey?

Betty Courmier was adamant that Joey's rehabilitation would proceed according to plan, whether Linda understood it or not. The plan was in Joey's best interest.

After Cherie's departure, there was much long-distance discussion between the two hospitals. Dr. Briggs talked to Dr. Zuker. As a result, Dr. Briggs became convinced that Joey was in capable hands.

On February 23, therapists, doctors, social workers, nurses and nutritionists met with Linda and Mike to discuss Joey's future.

Dr. Zuker presided at the meeting. He told Linda and Mike he did not think Joey would walk again, that he lacked the necessary motivation to try. That was why there was no therapy. He did not know about the knee; he would talk to an orthopedic surgeon. The special chair would be arriving within a week. Dr. Zuker added that he was considering sending Joey to a rehabilitation center before he went home — Joey was still too sick to be cared for at home.

It wasn't a pretty picture, but at least Linda and Mike knew where they stood. But Linda was still confused. If the doctors were right and Joey had reached his potential in the hospital, what good would rehabilitation do him? Would he receive extensive therapy in a rehabilitation center? Would it test the limits of his potential? How long would he need to be there? She didn't think he could stand much more time in a hospital. But what if taking him home jeopardized his future?

And what would she tell Joey now? He was losing his motivation. The nurses didn't push him, and he didn't want to participate. He complained about the food and the isolation. He said he was going crazy looking at the ceiling day after day.

The hospital convinced Linda and Mike that Joey would have to go to a rehabilitation center. Maybe he could go on weekends, or stay in one week, then go home for a week. They were waiting for a report from one of Ontario's best known rehabilitation centers, the Hugh MacMillan. The report shocked everyone. It stated flatly that Joey was not a good candidate for their center or for any other center in Canada. Hugh MacMillan could not accept patients with MRSA, and the center thought Joey was not sufficiently motivated to participate in their program.

Dr. Zuker suggested that the hospital could do no more for him and that Joey should be sent home. Linda worried that in Orillia he would not get the services he would need. She was especially concerned about physiotherapy. She asked the medical team at Sick Kids to make sure the community resources would be adequate.

Joey was largely free of pain. His arms were bandaged and splinted; they resembled two boomerangs sprouting from his shoulders. His legs were bandaged heavily to prevent infection. (The lower legs were still not covered with new skin.) He could raise and lower them with assistance. The feet were pointing downward, and if they remained in that position Joey would not be able to walk. He was depressed. He wanted more than anything else in the world to go home. Linda wanted nothing more than to take him there. But not yet. Not until she was clear that he would not suffer for it later.

A specially designed chair, which would allow Joey some mobility, arrived in mid-March. It was a great hulk of a thing, and it could roll down into a stretcher, incline at different levels or sit up like a normal wheelchair. It was Joey's ticket to freedom. The last time he had felt the winds of the planet sweep across him was on that long-ago day in Boston.

It was a cold wintry day, and Linda and Mike bundled Joey up in blankets and covered his face against the snow. Linda and Mike were told to go no farther than the front steps. They did stay at the front door for a while. They watched the cars going by and the people coming and going and the mountains of concrete rising up all around them. It wasn't all that exciting; Mike thought it wasn't enough. He asked Joey if he was hungry, then proposed a trip to the Eaton Centre for a snack.

Linda and Mike wheeled Joey across the road, then down University Avenue. They waited at the lights, laughing, telling Joey where they were and what was around him. Joey was laughing, too. He thought it was a hilarious adventure. Passing cars honked their horns. People stopped to watch the tiny entourage with the enormous chair. They heard laughter coming from somewhere beneath the covers.

At Dundas Street, Mike and Linda pushed the stretcher down the curb, then ran to beat the lights. Suddenly they got stuck in the streetcar tracks. The stretcher wouldn't budge. They pulled and twisted. The light turned yellow. They pulled some more. The light turned red. Joey was laughing. This was the biggest thrill he had had since he entered the hospital. When they finally got going, the drivers around them began honking and waving.

The vast shopping center was like a shot of adrenaline for Joey. It was filled with people and energy. He looked up from his stretcher chair to the enormous ceiling, way up above him, and saw the giant kitelike constructions shimmering under the dome. They went into a restaurant and ordered hamburgers and French fries. Joey wanted a milk shake. Then he told Linda he had to go to the washroom. Mike and Linda looked at each other, wondering how they would get seven long feet of chair into a public washroom. Joey looked at them, and they all broke out laughing. Linda went to survey the ladies' washroom. No one there. With Mike's help, she wheeled him in. On the way back to Sick Kids, they wheeled Joey along Yonge Street for a few blocks to give him a last taste of the city's manic energy.

It was a glorious afternoon.

MARTYN KENDRICK   147

In the first week of March, the medical team at the hospital decided Joey would be ready to go home within the next few weeks. Linda spoke to Ken McCan, who said everything could be ready by the beginning of April.

In the next few weeks there was intense activity in many quarters. Medical and social systems scrambled into gear, calling upon their ordinary resources to cope with an extraordinary homecoming. Nurses, physiotherapists, doctors, homemakers, ambulance services, the house builders and others worked separately and in collaboration to take Joey home and care for him. They set a date: April 3, 1989. Joey began counting the hours. He promised Linda he would work hard at home. He was happy and motivated. Linda took advantage of his mood to make a last-minute trip to Boston. She wanted to talk to the medical team at Shriners, to reassure herself that Joey would do all right at home, and to learn anything she could about the kind of care he would need. On her second day in Boston, she received a message to call Mike. It was marked "urgent."

As it turned out, four days before Joey was scheduled to go home, the medical team in Toronto had to change the plan. The team had been unable to find a GP willing to accept Joey as a patient. He would have to stay at Sick Kids until a doctor could be found. Dr. Clark had scheduled a meeting for Wednesday, April 5, at which he hoped the problem could be resolved.

Dr. Clark asked Mike to break the news to Joey. When he did, Joey began crying, loud, racking sobs. He was inconsolable.

On Monday evening, when she returned to Toronto, Linda went to see Joey. He had been waiting for her.

She sat at the edge of his bed and embraced him. Joey told her he had told one of the nurses he wouldn't like to be a nurse on the floor when his mother got back.

In the next few weeks, the hospital went to extremes to make Joey comfortable. And the Orillia medical community rallied to support its adopted son. Orillia's Victorian Order of Nurses would work in shifts to monitor and help with his nursing care. Susan, his primary nurse from Toronto, would spend a week with him at home, assessing his needs and establishing a home-care nursing plan.

By April 17, 1989, Orillia's medical community had finished transforming the new house into an active rehabilitation center.

Joey barely slept the night before his rescheduled departure. Nia spent the morning with him while Linda attended to last-minute details. A press conference was called for eleven o'clock, with doctors, therapists and social workers on hand to announce Joey's departure. Reporters from Boston, New York, and across Canada were on hand.

Dr. Clark told the reporters that Joey was a remarkable young man who had survived against all odds. The two skin-graft operations performed in Toronto had been only moderately successful, but Dr. Clark thought Joey's wounds might close on their own. He said Joey's body had powerful healing abilities. Once he was motivated to continue his therapy, Joey would gain limited independence. The doctors were not sure whether he would walk again. His knee had no bones, tendons or muscles to fuse with, but it was possible it would fuse on its own. Dr. Clark explained the hospital's plan to monitor Joey and check up on him twice a month.

Joey was wheeled out of the hospital at 11:16, his broad smile showing as swarms of reporters hovered around him. Nia, her long blond hair blowing, was standing by his side. She was afraid of flying, yet exhilarated at the same time. Joey calmed her fears. Then, at 11:37 AM, thirteen months and seven days after the fire, Joey Philion, the boy who had cheated death, was airborne. He was finally going home.

When the helicopter touched down in Orillia, hundreds of

people lined the runway. They were carrying huge signs and banners welcoming the hero home, and chanting "Welcome home, Joey" as they strained to catch a glimpse of him. As the nurses wheeled Joey off the helicopter, his broad smile told them all how grateful he was that they cared. He waved as he was transferred to the ambulance that would take him to Cleveland Avenue.

The crowd followed the ambulance. As Joey and his entourage pulled up to the house, hundreds more people were standing, clapping and crying. Joey, too, was crying — with happiness. Nia stood beside him, and Yoda, his new dog, was trying to get up on the stretcher. Wilson McTavish, the official guardian, received the house key from Ken McCan, then handed it to Joey, who in turn handed it to his mother. Joey waved again as he was wheeled in through the front doors.

They wheeled him past the sun-dappled sitting room, across the white tile floor and to the enormous living room. They stopped near the French doors that looked out onto the backyard. Then his nurses wheeled him to the elevator, went to the second floor and wheeled him to his bedroom, which was directly across from the elevator. They took him off the stretcher and placed him in his specially designed bed.

Downstairs, Nia, Peter and Bran, Rhian (Nia's younger sister), Linda, Mike, Danny and special friends were celebrating. Bran had brought two chickens. Linda found vegetables in the cupboards the community had stocked. Peter brought out wine and Mike brought out champagne and they prepared a feast.

When it was ready, Mike and Tim carried Joey downstairs and set him on the couch, and Yoda jumped up and licked his face. They sang songs and laughed. Linda thought she was dreaming.

They drank a toast to Joey, to friendship and to the future, and Linda allowed Joey to have a thimbleful of champagne.

He toasted with them and laughed as he not laughed in a long time.

The next day two technicians arrived to demonstrate the custom-made electric wheelchair-cum-stretcher that they were designing for Joey. They showed him how it worked. He was giddy with excitement when he saw it. He turned himself nearly upside down, twisted it to the side and wheeled it back and forth across the floor. It was the first time he had been able to do anything for himself in more than a year.

The routine Joey would follow for at least a year was quickly established. Two nurses and a physiotherapist arrived each morning at eight o'clock to change his dressing and help him exercise. Then they transferred him, in a specially designed lift, to his custom-made tub for a bath. Homemakers came three times a week to help Linda with the chores and to give her a break. Within weeks Joey's range of motion increased three-fold. His nurses were amazed. And his leg began to heal, as the doctors in Toronto had hoped. Within two months he was doing situps and lifting his legs without pain for the first time since the accident. His main medical problem now is his hands. Underneath the splints the palms of his hands became badly infected. They are raw and painful. Neither Dr. Cormode, his family doctor, nor his nurses have a solution.

His will is still strong. In the near future, Dr. John Simmington, whose work in assisting the handicapped achieve independence is legendary, will be visiting Joey. With Joey's will and Dr. Simmington's knowledge, there is much hope.

Joey Philion's recovery has come about at enormous cost. Shriners underwrote the cost of his treatment in Boston — three million dollars. The Ontario Health Insurance Plan (OHIP) paid for three quarters of the cost of his treatment in Toronto. His bed and basic nursing care at Toronto's Hospital for Sick Children cost almost six hundred thousand dollars.

The home-care nursing, the special creams and medications

and doctor's fees cost about four hundred dollars a day. (Seventy-five percent is paid by OHIP.) His equipment, including the custom-made electric wheelchair, the lift, the bath and his specially designed bed, cost about forty thousand dollars.

To save Joey Philion's life has cost about four million dollars to date. To keep him alive will cost about one hundred fifty thousand dollars a year.

The Hawkinses are expected to pay a quarter of the total cost of care.

Joey has a VCR in his bedroom, and there is a satellite dish on the roof that allows him to get hundreds of stations. They were gifts that came with the house. In the basement, boxes are filled with gifts and letters and awards and tributes from around the world. These gifts represent the desire of thousands of people to fuel Joey's dreams. Joey needs to dream again.

Joey's life is not easy. A few of his old friends come to the house now and again, but they don't know what to say. When they leave, Joey watches through the window as they get on their bikes and ride away to play the games he can no longer play. He knows the limits of his body. He tries to walk with assistance but it's hard. He knows he might be confined to a wheelchair for the rest of his life.

Linda smiles, but there is pain in her eyes, too. She knows how independent he was, and she must look at him, confined to his bed and chair, dependent upon her and Mike and a team of medical specialists. She can't stand to see him in any kind of pain. Joey, sensitive to her unspoken conflicts, refuses to let her in the room when he is suffering in any way. The stress of the last year has weakened her. She wonders if the pain in her heart will ever go away.

The future of course is uncertain, but trends are surfacing which merge Joey's private and public worlds.

Joey is frequently asked by a variety of organizations to

speak with their members about his ordeal. At one conference, sponsored by YTV, Toronto, where he received an award for bravery, over one thousand people spontaneously stood and cheered as Joey approached the podium. They continued clapping for nearly ten minutes. He then spoke quietly and clearly about love, suffering, tragedy and triumph in simple terms that were rendered all the more moving because he embodied the ideas he trumpeted. When he left the stage and returned with Nia to his family's side, young and old alike came up to shake his hand and thank him profusely. This response is repeated over and over again wherever he goes. Initially he was unsure how to respond to the people he met. But he has become progressively more comfortable with this public role. Indeed he seems to have found a purpose in his appearances: to let others use the example of his courage and suffering, the worst of which is behind him, as a way to meaning.

Linda and Mike dream of establishing a rehabilitation centre on Vancouver Island — an area Joey loves — which would serve as a place of refuge for families of burn victims. Based on their experiences, and enlisting the aid and expertise of the Shriners and others in the field, they hope to begin work on it in the near future. Linda says it would be one way of responding to the many people who helped them through their ordeal while also giving them a sense of purpose.

Nia often takes Joey for long walks along the country roads surrounding his home, ending up at the edge of the nearby lake. Joey will sit there for hours looking out over the water, losing himself in the landscape. He doesn't say what he thinks about during these increasingly common contemplative moments. Nia says he still dreams of flying. Ultimately, he must search within himself to find the vision that will free his soul, suggest his future and make him happy to be alive. . . again.

INDEX

INDEX

air ambulance, 44-45, 115,
 120, 148
Air Cadets, 16-18, 125
Anne, mother of Brian,
 108
Anne, receptionist, 112
Arlene, friend, 37
artificial skin, 56
autografts, 56, 61-62

Beselt, Commander
 Dennis, 113-14
Bird, Larry, 91
blood donors, 68
Boy Scouts, 125
Bradley, Dr., 67-69
Brett, friend of Joey's,
 114
Brian, burn victim,
 108-109
Briggs, Dr. Susan, 49, 53,
 59, 65, 68, 76, 98-99,
 145; and Joey's
 treatment, 56-57
Bruins T-shirt, 114
burns, degrees of, 36
Buysky, Dr. Jo, 73-74

calcium growths, 105-106,
 109
Camille, father of Brian,
 108

Campbell River, 11
Canadian Snowbirds,
 113-14
Cartigainer, Pat, 50
CBC, 121, 139
Cherie, night nurse, 103,
 111, 143
Children's Aid Society,
 105
Christmas Day, 1988,
 138-39
CKVR television, 121
Clark, Dr., plastic
 surgeon, 43-44, 122,
 129, 147-48
Cleveland Avenue: and
 electrical system, 19;
 heating of, 13-14; move
 to, 12; site, 82, 127
Colonial Homes, 82
Cooke, Wayne, Jr., 16-17,
 31, 70-72
Cooke, Wayne, Sr., 16, 31
Cormode, Dr., family
 doctor, 150
cost of treatment, 83,
 150-51
Courmier, Betty, 123, 126,
 133, 143-44

Day, Jeff, 79, 119, 121
debridement, 37, 49
Dermabrader, 61
Dermatone, 61

155

Lion's Club, 82

McCan, Dan, 130-31, 141
McCan, Delsie, 126-28, 140
McCan, Ken, 126-28, 140, 147, 149
McMurtry, Roy, 143
McTavish, Wilson, 149
Marilyn, Danny's foster mother, 107
Massachusetts General Hospital, 52-53, 107
Mattel toys, 69
media, 69-70, 85-86, 119-23, 131
medical expenses, 83, 150-51
medical treatment, 30, 35, 37, 59-64, 96, 103-107, 109-11
Michael, Father, 97-98, 113
Monica, primary nurse, 102
MRSA, 124, 129, 132, 145
Mulroney, Brian, 91, 113

Nancy, pain nurse, 109

Ontario Health Insurance Plan (OHIP), 150
Orillia, move to, 12
Orillia *Packet and Times*, 70, 79, 119, 121
Orillia Soldier's Memorial Hospital, 28-30
Orr, Bobby, 91

pain control, 37, 42, 58-60, 74, 97, 100, 103, 107,141, 150
Parfect, John, 138-39
Pavulon, 65, 69, 71
Philion, Andy, father of Joey, 9, 38; and customs officials, 55
Philion, Danny: in Boston, 73; and foster home, 105, 107; and Joey, 8-9, 39-40; personal characteristics, 18, 81, 142;
Philion, Joey: burn damage, 35-36; characteristics, 18; day of fire, 24-27; Linda's presence, 42-43, 75; and love of flying, 9; medical condition, 50-51, 56, 67, 96,

watch, as talisman, 32, 41
water pipes, 14-15
Wayne, John, 51
wheelchair, 145-46, 150-51
Wilkes, Jim, 90, 137
Wilma, neighbor, 27, 32, 33
Wood, Trish, 121, 139

Yoda, the dog, 149
Young, Doug, 26-27, 33
Young, Linda, 32-33, 128-29; day of fire, 25-27, 29
YTV, Toronto, 152

Zuker, Dr. Joe, 34, 129, 132, 144

ABOUT THE AUTHOR

Martyn Kendrick is the author of the critically-acclaimed *Anatomy of a Nightmare: The Failure of Society in Dealing with Child Sexual Abuse*, which appeared on the Coles national bestseller list for several weeks. He lives with his wife and daughter in Hamilton.